Theoretical Aspects
of
Roman Camp and Fort Design

Theoretical Aspects of Roman Camp and Fort Design

Alan Richardson

BAR International Series 1321
2004

Published in 2016 by
BAR Publishing, Oxford

BAR International Series 1321

Theoretical Aspects of Roman Camp and Fort Design

© A Richardson and the Publisher 2004

Volume Editor: John W Hedges

The author's moral rights under the 1988 UK Copyright,
Designs and Patents Act are hereby expressly asserted.

All rights reserved. No part of this work may be copied, reproduced, stored,
sold, distributed, scanned, saved in any form of digital format or transmitted
in any form digitally, without the written permission of the Publisher.

ISBN 9781841713908 paperback
ISBN 9781407327488 e-format
DOI https://doi.org/10.30861/9781841713908
A catalogue record for this book is available from the British Library

BAR Publishing is the trading name of British Archaeological Reports (Oxford) Ltd.
British Archaeological Reports was first incorporated in 1974 to publish the BAR
Series, International and British. In 1992 Hadrian Books Ltd became part of the BAR
group. This volume was originally published by John and Erica Hedges Ltd. in
conjunction with British Archaeological Reports (Oxford) Ltd / Hadrian Books Ltd,
the Series principal publisher, in 2004. This present volume is published by BAR
Publishing, 2016.

BAR titles are available from:

        BAR Publishing
        122 Banbury Rd, Oxford, OX2 7BP, UK
EMAIL info@barpublishing.com
PHONE +44 (0)1865 310431
FAX +44 (0)1865 316916
        www.barpublishing.com

CONTENTS

Contents		i
Preface		1
1.	The origins of the Roman camp	3
2.	Camps of the late Republic	11
3.	The camp of the imperial army	21
4.	Forts, fortlets and legionary fortresses	35
5.	The forts of the frontier walls	51
6.	The deployment of Roman armies in the field	55
7.	General discussion	67
Appendix One: Hyginus, *De Munitionibus Castrorum* (in English)		69
Appendix Two: Some Roman camps in Britain		79
Appendix Three: An algorithm for Roman military granaries		83
Bibliography		85
Index		89

PREFACE

This book is not a history of the Roman army, nor a full review of its technology. It is about the theoretical basis of the planning of Roman camps and forts, a field of interest to the author which has resulted in six published papers (Richardson 1997, 2000, 2001, 2002, 2003, 2004). These papers were somewhat tedious since they attempted to extract the general rules for making camps and forts from the disparate information found in ancient texts and modern archaeological reports. The method was necessarily inductive and involved some simple statistics and computer modelling.

These findings are now presented in a way that, hopefully, will be easier to follow and therefore more palatable to the average student of Roman military history. Nevertheless, a certain amount of numerical data must be confronted because it is of the very nature of the subject. These data have been taken from the relevant publications, or derived from them by calculation. They cannot be absolutely accurate, given the drawings' scales, but neither are they to be dismissed on that account, nor the reasonable inferences drawn from them. For ease of reading, citations of the author's previous papers have been kept to a minimum, though this has resulted in some apparently sweeping statements. The reader wishing to challenge them is referred to the original publications. A certain amount of new material is also included.

I have also included a translation of Hyginus's *De Munitionibus Castrorum* made by Sir Ian Richmond for his friend F.G. Simpson, because there is not a published version available in English. This was kindly made available to me by Dr Grace Simpson. It is also a pleasure to acknowledge the help of Dr Brian Dobson who has provided me with much useful information and comment over several years. I also owe thanks to the late Prof. Oswald Dilke and to Dr Martin Henig for their support and encouragement.

Alan Richardson, 16, Thorpe Field, Sockbridge, Penrith, Cumbria, CA10 2JN

April 2004

CHAPTER ONE

THE ORIGINS OF THE ROMAN CAMP

Introduction

Roman camps, sometimes called *marching*, or *summer*, camps because of their short period of use are among the most impressive and enigmatic of ancient monuments, yet they are nothing more than rectangular enclosures bounded by a rampart and ditch. The simple construction has meant that very few of those that must have been made are now known. Some have been long recognised; most notably those associated with the siege works at Numantia in Spain and at Masada, Israel. Both these groups were investigated in the early years of the last century by the German scholar, Adolf Schulten, while in Britain, General Roy was the first to study those that could be seen in the 18th century on the open lands of northern England and Scotland. During the 20th century, aerial photography in Britain, most notably by Prof. St Joseph, has revealed many more, now destroyed by agriculture. The camps in England have been described in detail by Welfare and Swan (1995).

In contrast to temporary camps, the remains of permanent forts have tended to persist due to their more robust construction, and many lost sites have been rediscovered by modern archaeology. Most cover less than ten acres but some reach to over thirty; while legionary fortresses may extend to more than 50 acres. At the other extreme, some forts are small enough to be regarded as fortlets. There were many similarly small camps. But all these structures were based on the same conceptual plan; a rectangular outline with straight sides and rounded corners; the gates placed in the sides and not at the corners.

Our information on the camp's internal arrangements comes from three main sources; Polybius (c. 200 – 118 BC), Josephus author of the *Jewish War* (born AD 37) and a certain Hyginus who lived at some time during the late empire. Polybius described in detail the camp of a two-legion consular army that he must have seen about 160 BC. Josephus saw the imperial Roman army at work in Palestine and though no military expert, he gave a good account of its awesome efficiency. Hyginus's treatise, *De munitionibus castrorum,* gives considerable detail about the organisation of the imperial army and its camp, but his precise date is uncertain. Some scholars have placed him as early as Hadrian, but he must be much later because he was commissioned to discover how to make a camp from the available literature, as if the task had become a lost art. His report contains considerable, and undoubtedly accurate, detail but in a vague and rambling format. Moreover, he could not discover the principles of how the site was surveyed, or the camp laid out; and his didactic style, even when he is thin on the facts, is typical civil servants' bluff. He probably wrote in late imperial times and if this was the best that could be done, the loss of know-how was already fatal. Hyginus's master would have found the report more or less useless. The same might be said of Vegetius who is thought to have flourished in the late 4th century AD (Milner 1993). His work, *Epitome of Military Science*, is a crude summary of the Roman military achievement, and though valuable to us, it could not have served as an instruction manual.

Early Roman armies

The army of the early Roman republic was apparently based on a mass of infantrymen formed into a phalanx, but about 360 BC it was re-modelled into a more open battle order (Keppie 1984). The men in the new model legion were organised according to their social and political status and since the *centuria*, a division of a voting tribe, numbered 100 men, the first legions probably comprised of 100-strong centuries. The cavalry were drawn from the equestrian order but not in sufficient numbers, so Rome became reliant on her allies for horsemen.

Field Fortifications

The army of the republic perfected the art of *field fortification*, a technology that principally involves making fortified camps but perhaps should, strictly speaking, include any form of trenching and embanking for tactical purposes. This stratagem in some form must have been widely practised during many ages, at least on a pragmatic basis, but by the time of the Peloponnesian war, the Greeks were capable of making both siege-walls and defensive entrenchments on a large scale, the Athenians notably employing both at the siege of Syracuse (415 BC).

But siege works are not the same as trenching and banking to defend the temporary camp sites of armies in the field and the Greeks first made the distinction. According to Polybius, they fortified their camps by adapting the local terrain to the defence. The Greeks, he wrote, "…think above all of the security they can achieve by exploiting the natural strength of the position, first because they grudge the labour involved in entrenching, and secondly because they think man-made defences are inferior to those provided by the natural features of the site. And so as regards the plan of the camp as a whole they are compelled to adopt all kinds of shapes so as to conform to the lie of the ground…"

Whatever principles informed the Greek methods they did not amount to a system, or paradigm, that could be applied under all circumstances but about the turn of the third century BC, the Greek king, Pyrrhus of Epirus (319 – 272 BC), made a major innovation that induced Hannibal (247 – 182 BC), in his prickly interview with Scipio, to rate him second only to Alexander the Great as a general. This was almost certainly a standardised method of camp fortification that was a significant advance on the traditional *ad hoc* entrenching the site. Another tradition, however, maintains that, meanwhile, the Romans had developed their own system so that when Pyrrhus first saw them digging-in some time before the battle at Heraclea in 280 BC, he realised they were not the barbarians he had expected.

The Roman camp plan

It seems, therefore, that about 300 BC, the Romans had already developed a method of camp fortification. There is no direct evidence of how they approached the problem but the features of their later camps give some clues to the original thinking. They seem to have started from the basic premise that in defending one's ground in the harsh world of hand-to-hand combat, it was better to stand upon an elevated position behind an obstacle that impeded the enemy. This was not revolutionary, since simple earthen banks and ditches are features of many pre-historic settlements. But to this simple device the Romans applied a clear understanding of the quantitative aspects of the effort involved in making and defending them. They seemed to have measured the amount of work that an infantryman could do without tiring himself out and used it to inform the design of the camp and then fix the composition of their infantry units.

Their camp model required their military engineers to resolve the conflict between having the shortest possible defensive perimeter with having enough room within the camp. The more densely the men were packed-in, the shorter would be the perimeter. But this would mean less space for pitching tents and moving about, leading to crowding and confusion. In short, they faced a trade-off between the numbers of men per unit area and the numbers of men per unit length of perimeter, and the design had to strike the right balance.

The shortest perimeter for any given area is given by a circle and no doubt circular camps were considered, and perhaps even tried. But the internal arrangements within a circular camp would present problems because there would be only one fixed datum point from which all measurements for defining the useable space could be made, the centre. This would be extremely awkward, if not impossible.

The next most convenient outline was the square, which provides two sides, or axes (plural of axis), by which the internal space can be defined. This was, in fact, the ideal Greek town plan originated by Hippodamus of Miletus in the 5th century BC and widely copied throughout the ancient Mediterranean world (Dilke 1971). It had a grid of streets based on two central roads that crossed at right angles and this was the model chosen by the Romans. The camp would therefore be rectangular with a street grid based on the cross roads, the tents being pitched in the side streets. It would be confined by a defensive perimeter consisting of a rampart (*vallum*) and an outer ditch (*fossa*). This perimeter would be set at some distance from the tented area to allow for organising the defence and the intervening space would be known as the *intervallum*. Thus, the camp was like a mounted picture; the tented area lying within a margin bounded by an outer frame. See Figure 1.1. There is no direct evidence of any experimental project to produce such a design, nor can we be sure that this was the sort of camp seen by Pyrrhus, but the features of later camps suggest it was.

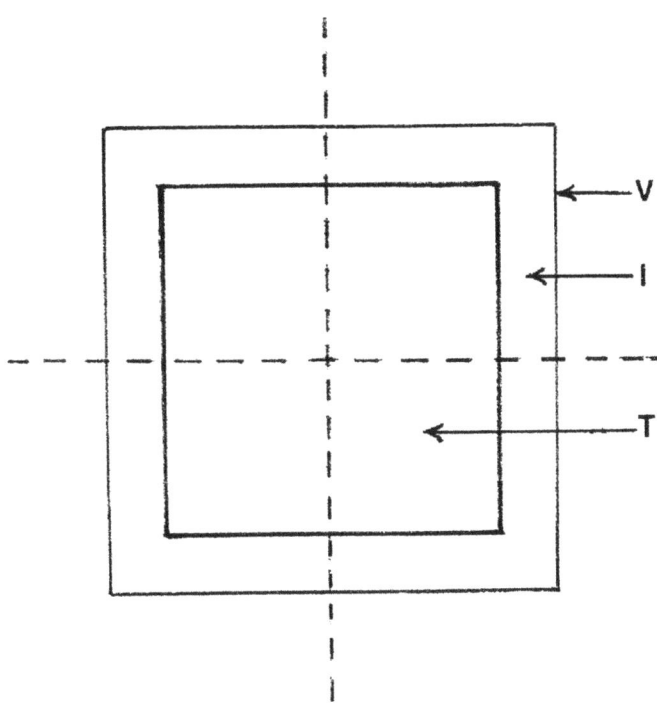

FIGURE 1.1: BASIC FEATURES OF THE CAMP PLAN

(V = Vallum and ditch: I = Intervallum: T = Tented area)

The basic design task was therefore to define the rule for calculating the camp's dimensions from the numbers of men available. For reasons that will become clear, the basic planning exercise was almost certainly performed with the smallest infantry unit, the century, with the intent of scaling-up the model. With hand-held weapons, each man could command the ground immediately in front of him, but not more. A line of men spaced neither too close together nor too far apart would probably be placed at outstretched arms' length intervals, which is the same distance as the average man's height; about five and a half feet. A closer spacing would hamper arm movements and a wider one would allow gaps to occur. It seems the planners started from this basic premise and applied it to the century of 100 men. When placed within a square, the century would have 25 men to each side. Spaced six feet apart they would occupy 150 feet and at five feet apart they would take up 125 feet. At four feet intervals they would take up 100 feet. If the side of the square were the standard Roman land surveying unit, the *actus* of 120 feet, then each man would have had 4.8 feet of perimeter; only 2.5 inches short of five feet, and the area enclosed would be one *actus quadratus* (*a.q.*) or 14,400 sq. feet. But with such a square, a century of 80 men (20 per side) would have six feet of perimeter apiece.

A spacing of five to six feet per man had implications for the physical effort needed to dig the ditch and make the rampart. According to modern military engineering data, an infantryman could shift 0.5 cubic metres (17.66 cu. feet) of earth per hour (Peddie 1996-7, 151). Let us suppose a Roman soldier could manage 20 cu. feet. Each foot length of a V-section ditch, five feet wide and three feet deep, would account for 7.5 cu. feet of earth, so a six feet section would require the removal of 45 cu. feet of earth and take one man 45 / 20 = 2.25 hours. If the up-cast were used for the rampart, which would need turf facing to contain the spoil, a similar period of further work might be required. Four and half hours hard labour before a defensive fight was perhaps as much as a prudent general could allow.*

The next matter was the *intervallum*. It had to be wide enough to allow for movements between the rampart and the tents but not cramp the tented area. It had therefore to be *proportional* to the area enclosed; that is, some convenient fraction of the side of the square. The fraction chosen was 1/10th of the length of the rampart at its inner face, or 1/8th of the length of the *intervallum's* inner margin. The inter-relationship of these fractions was inherent in the model, as can be seen from Figure 1.2, which shows the partition of space within the camp; there are eight squares along the inner face of the *intervallum* and ten along the outside.

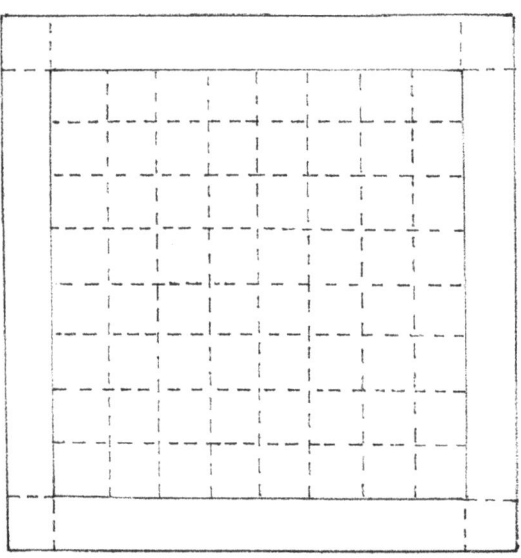

FIGURE 1.2: THE PARTITION OF SPACE WITHIN A CAMP

(Note the area within the intervallum is taken up by 8 x 8 sub-squares)

This is the template for all later Roman camps and forts, though the details of the model changed over time. It is a rectangle whose area (R) is defined by the inner face of the rampart with the *intervallum* some fraction (1/f) of the square root of R. This is also 1 / (f -2) of the square root of the area within the

---

* The tradition that each man should entrench and defend his own body length was recorded at Manchester in the 10th century (Crofton 1885)

intervallum (A). Outside the rampart there was a short space (berm) and then the ditch. The width and height of the rampart, as well as the depth and width of the ditch, would vary according to situation.

The essential features of three possible prototype squares for 100 infantry are shown in Table 1.1. Which option was the best? A clue comes from the area (A) which comprised the area actually occupied by the tents (T) and the remaining space for storing kit and the centurion's tent (A – T). The area (T) was made a simple fraction of (A). In the first camp for which we have dimensions, that described by Polybius, (T) was 5/6ths of (A) and gave each infantryman 83.33 sq. feet of tent-space. The area (A) of the third option (Table 1.1) gives each man 100 sq. feet within the *intervallum*. If 5/6ths of this were for his tent space, then he too would have had 83.33 sq. feet. This suggests that here we have the early model. Since T = 5/6 A, it follows that A = 6/5 T.

TABLE 1.1: CAMP MODELS FOR A CENTURY

(Lengths in feet: Areas in sq. feet)

Side of square	perimeter per man	Area within rampart (R)	*Intervallum* width	Side of tented area within *intervallum*	Area within *intervallum* (A)
100	4.0	10,000	10.0	80	6,400
120	4.8	14,400	12.0	96	9,216
125	5.0	15,625	12.5	100	10,000

The paradigm, explained this way, begins with the perimeter and works back to the area per man. But once the system was in operation those laying out the camp needed to calculate the area and dimensions starting with the numbers of men. The steps would have been as follows:

1. Number of men, or units, x space allowance = T (total area of the tents)
2. T x 6/5 = A (area within the *intervallum*)
3. L (side of the square) = $\sqrt{A}$
4. I (width of *intervallum*) = $1/8^{th} \sqrt{A}$
5. Rampart length of one side = L + 2I

Cavalry

A cavalryman and his horse obviously needed more space than an infantryman so he was given four times the space of the infantryman and in calculations counted as four infantrymen. This suggests a cavalry squadron (*turma*) may have originally comprised 25 men and occupied the same space as 100 infantry.

Influence of land surveying technology

The rectangular camp was set out from the point where the two axes crossed at right-angles. This procedure was almost certainly due to the application of land-surveying techniques borrowed from the Greeks, and perhaps also the Etruscans.

In a typical Roman land survey, two long axes, the *cardo maximus* and the *decumanus maximus* were set out at right-angles using the *groma*, a staff bearing crossed arms set at right angles and from whose extremities plumb bobs were suspended. From the base-lines, a matrix of secondary lines (*limites*) was laid out in a regular pattern so that the land was divided into a grid of squares. These were identified by co-ordinates related to the base lines. The unit of length was the *actus* (120 Roman feet of 11.65 inches) and the area measure was the *actus quadratus* (*a.q.*) of 120 x 120 Roman feet. The plots, or *centuriae*, were normally 20 x 20 *actus*. The whole process was known as *centuriation* and was the professional responsibility of land surveyors, or *agrimensores*, or *gromatici*. These men surveyed and mapped land, both private and state, set out boundaries and prepared official documentation. The subject has been reviewed by Prof. Oswald Dilke (1971) and more recently by Dr Brian Campbell (2000).

The first clue to the application of *agrimensorial* technology in camp lay-out comes from Hyginus. "On the main street, at the middle of the entrance to the *praetorium*," he writes (12), "is the point called *locus gromae*, either because the crowd collects there, or because in the laying out of the bounds, when the iron-shod upright has been placed on the spot, the *groma* is put thereon, that the gates of the camp may form the four quarters in range of the line. And the professional followers of this art are called *gromatici* for the reason given above."

The second clue is the term *decumanus* attached both to the long axis of a survey and to the posterior portion of the central axis of the camp. Dilke (1971, 231) discussed its likely origin, accepting that it referred to number ten but suggesting it was an augur's term for the main street of a town. He rejected Hyginus's notion that it was derived from the tenth legionary cohort which occupied the rear of a legionary camp and concluded, somewhat doubtfully, that it simply meant "large". In conversation with the author, he speculated that it was accurately translated as the "tenth hand" but felt this gave no insight into its origin. Vegetius (1.23) wrote that soldiers to be punished were taken out by the back gate so the term might refer to decimation, the execution of every tenth man in a mutinous or disgraced unit.

The third clue comes from the dimensions of subdivisions within the Hyginian camp; they are all multiples or simple fractions of 120 feet. This was not the case with the camp described by Polybius, yet as will be shown, the *actus* is detectable in its conceptual plan.

Larger camps

It was an integral feature of the paradigm that with larger armies no man would labour upon and defend more than five to six feet of perimeter. Indeed he would have much less labouring to do. This is due to the geometric properties of a square whose perimeter does not increase at the same rate as its area. Consider three squares thus;

Area	Side	Perimeter (sum of sides)
4	$\sqrt{4} = 2.0$	8.0
8	$\sqrt{8} = 2.8$	11.3
16	$\sqrt{16} = 4.0$	16.0

As the area is quadrupled (4 to 16) the perimeter is only doubled (8 to 16). This means that as the army and its camp increased, relatively more men became available for the perimeter. It could therefore be made more quickly with more men to defend it. In very large camps there was ample labour to make and defend very substantial ramparts. With 4,000 men there was 0.8 feet of perimeter per man. See Table 1.2.

TABLE 1.2: CAMP AREA AND PERIMETER IN RELATION TO THE NUMBERS OF INFANTRY

Centuries	Men	Area (sq. ft.)	Perimeter (ft.)	Perimeter per man (ft.)
1	100	15,625	500	5.0
5	500	78,122	1,118	2.2
20	2,000	312,488	2,236	1.1
40	4,000	624,975	3,162	0.8

Calculating camp dimensions

It was easy to calculate the camp's dimensions as the number of centuries increased. Each needed 10,000 feet within the *intervallum*. If dimensions were measured in 10 feet units, allowing the use of ten-foot measuring rods, the *decempedae*, the area per century within the *intervallum* (A) would be 100 sq. *decempedae*, i.e., A = centuries x 100. The side of the square would be $\sqrt{A}$, or ten *decempedae*. So for 5 centuries, the side of the square is $\sqrt{(5 \times 100)}$ = 22.3 *decempedae*; or 223 feet. To this must be added the *intervallum* which is $1/8^{th}$ of 223, or 28 feet, giving a dimension at the inner face of the rampart of 223 + (2 x 28) = 279 feet.

If we consider a legion of say 4,000 men (40 centuries) together with 250 cavalry (equivalent to 10 centuries) then the side of the square within the *intervallum* would be $\sqrt{(50 \times 100)}$ = 70.7 *decempedae*, or 707 feet. A force of two legions plus an equal number of allies would be four times greater; 200 centuries, and the calculation would be $\sqrt{(200 \times 100)}$ = 141.4 *decempedae*, or 1,414 feet. The *intervallum* would be then be added to define the inner face of the rampart; that is extended at each end by $1/8^{th}$ of its length, to give 1,414 + (2 x 176.75) or 1,767.5 feet.

Again, there is no direct evidence that this sort of calculation was ever made; but it is difficult to see how variously sized camps could have been made without something like it. A reasonably competent engineer with a table of square roots and a few measuring roads, or even five-foot spears, would have had no problem. It is, however, more than likely that the dimensions for various camps were calculated by the staff and set out in tables or learned parrot fashion by the responsible officer, the *praefectus castrorum*, who directed the *metatores* who actually measured out the camp.

This raises the question of Roman mathematics. Ancient Greek mathematicians were very competent. They worked out a great deal of geometry and arithmetic, including multiplication, division and decimals. They also understood square roots, many of whose values had already been calculated by the Babylonians and Egyptians. Much of Greek mathematics was at least at modern GCE 'A' level standard and much of it was available to the educated Roman. There can be no doubt that the sort of calculations involved in setting out camps posed no problem. By the time of the late republic, the Romans were using a special system of shorthand with a duodecimal system of fractions, i.e., based on twelfths with a half written as 6/12 and a quarter as 3/12. This would have suited calculations with 120 feet units (*actus*) for the *decempeda* was a twelfth of an *actus*. Moreover, as we shall see, Greek notions of mathematical harmony were integral to the paradigm as it evolved. For a full treatment of ancient mathematics, see Heath (1921) and Dilke (1987).

The evolution of the camp paradigm

The organisation of the army and its order of battle were obviously dictated by tactical considerations but they also reflected the social realities of the republic during the last centuries BC. Changes in both these areas influenced military organisation. The evolutionary process is not easy to reconstruct from the surviving fragments of information; Livy informs us that at one time a legion comprised 5,000 infantry and 300 cavalry while the legions known to Polybius comprised 4,200 infantry and 300 cavalry. Marius (*circa* 100 BC) adopted a legion of 6,000 and amalgamated the centuries into cohorts (Keppie 1998, 63). But whatever the numbers and method of organisation, the camp paradigm could cope. Thus, for a square camp, the axis, or side at the *inner margin* of the *intervallum*, was the square root of the sum of all the space allocations of the men (or units). It could be written as a general formula:

$$\text{Side or axis} = \sqrt{(s\ n\ m)} \quad \text{where}$$

s = the space needed by a unit; be it century, maniple or cohort;
n = number of such units, having converted cavalry to infantry equivalents;
m = the value by which the tented area is multiplied to give the space within the *intervallum*, i.e. 6/5 in the camps noted thus far, and hereafter referred to as the "multiplier".

The *intervallum* was $1/8^{th}$ the side of the square.

*****

CHAPTER TWO

CAMPS OF THE LATE REPUBLIC

Polybius

Polybius (c. 200 -118 BC) wrote to explain to his fellow Greeks how Rome had become the dominant Mediterranean power. He particularly stressed the Roman attitude to war – they trained constantly and left nothing to chance. In Book VI he gave a detailed account of the camp made by a consular army comprising two legions and allies (*socii*) but did not cite his sources though he must have obtained his information from a military manual or from some competent officer. His description is quite empirical; there is no hint of principles and all dimensions are simply stated in feet. He mentioned a formula that was invariably applied, but did not give it.

The consular army described by Polybius

Despite the absence of any reference to underlying theory, Polybius disclosed several clues that suggest that both the army and camp he saw were modifications of an earlier model. The infantry comprised two legions, each of 4,200 men with an equal number of allies, whilst the cavalry comprised 600 legionaries and 1,800 allies, all organised in *turmae* of 30. See Table 2.1.

TABLE 2.1

THE CONSULAR ARMY OF POLYBIUS

	Legionary	Allied	Totals
Infantry	8,400	8,400	16,800
Cavalry	600	1,800	2,400
Totals	9,000	10,200	19,200

The infantry appear to have been organised in basic units of 60, recombined in certain proportions, thus:

Triarii, 60-men units.
Principes, 120 (2 x 60) men units.
Hastati, 120 (2 x 60) men units.
Peditates Sociorum (allies) 240 (4 x 60) units.

Each legion therefore comprised 70 (4,200 / 60) basic units that probably represent centuries reduced from 100 to 60 men. The cavalry *turmae* of 30 may, as has been suggested above, represent an increase of five over an original 25. These five needed the space of 20 infantrymen so the reduction in infantry numbers per century might be related to enlarged *turmae*; the loss of 40 men from each century released space for 10 cavalry.

The camp described by Polybius

The camp was a square with sides of 2,017 feet and an *intervallum* of 200 feet, which is within 20 inches of $1/10^{th}$ of 2,017 feet. The area at the rampart was 282.5 *a.q.* and that within the *intervallum* 181.6 *a.q.* The partition was almost 280 to 180, but not quite. The area of the *intervallum* was 100.9 *a.q* (282.5 – 181.6). The proportions are almost 180 *a.q.* within the *intervallum*; 280 *a.q.* at the rampart and an *intervallum* of 100 *a.q.*

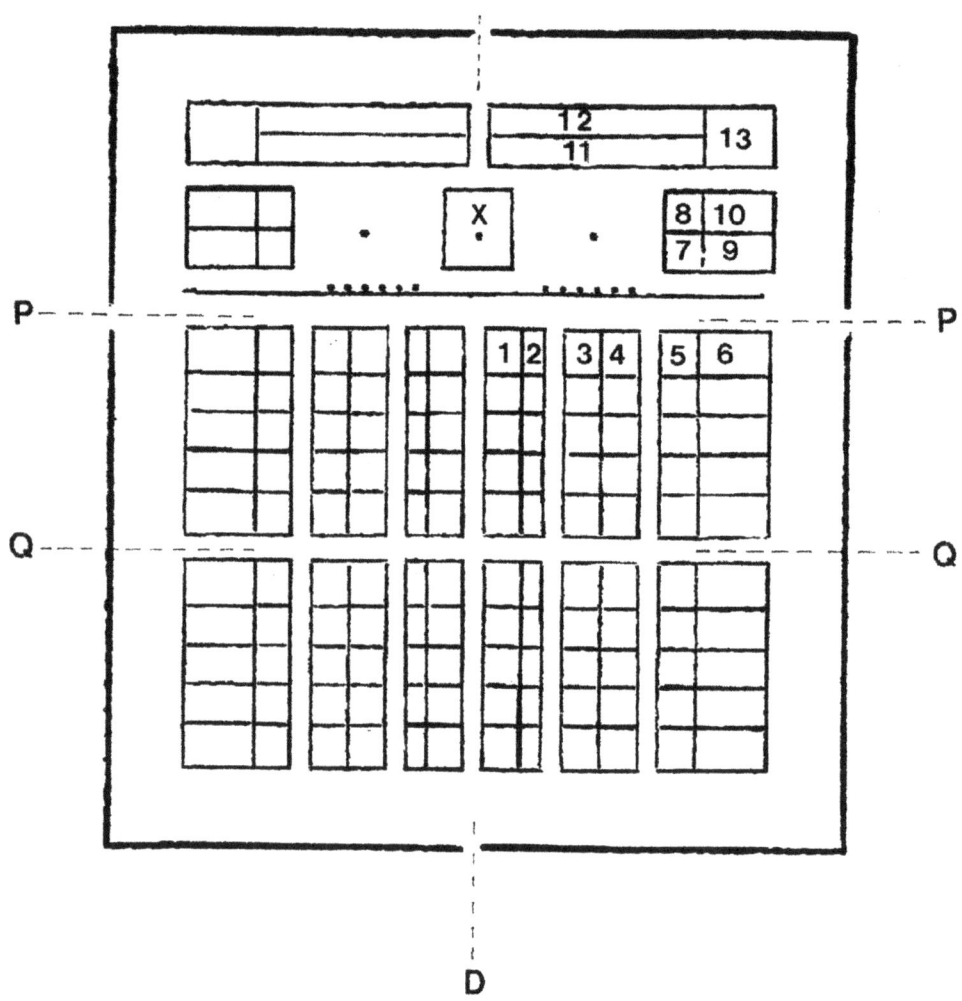

FIGURE 2.1

THE POLYBIAN CAMP

(After Ramsey and Lanciani 1901, 447-450: Gate at the top is the Porta Praetoria: D = Porta decumana: P = Principia: Q = Via Quintana: For the key to numbers 1 to 10, see Table 2.2: X = Praetorium: 8 to 10 = Tents of the legionary staff: 11 = Allied cavalry: 12 = Allied infantry: 13 = Irregular troops)

Within the *intervallum* the men's tents, laid out in orderly rows, occupied separate areas according to unit. These areas were measured in feet. The whole camp was divided into three parts by two lateral streets; a main one, the *Principia*, and a lesser, the *Via Quintana*, while a longitudinal axis divided it into two halves. The *Principia*, was 100 feet wide and the *Via Quintana* was 50 feet wide. Since the *intervallum* was 200 feet wide, this might suggest general rule that the *principia* should be half the *intervallum* and the *Via Quintana*, a quarter of it. Figure 2.1 shows these arrangements.

Table 2.2 details the allocation of space within the tent blocks below the *Principia* where the bulk of the troops camped.

TABLE 2.2

SPACE ALLOCATION IN THE POLYBIAN CAMP

Block	Area (sq. feet)	Soldier type	Numbers per block	Area per man (sq. feet)	
1	10,000	Legionary cavalry	30		333.33
2	5,000	Triarii	60	83.33	
3	10,000	Principes	120	83.33	
4	10,000	Hastati	120	83.33	
5	13,300	Allied cavalry	40		332.5
6	20,000	Allied infantry	240	83.33	

It is important to note:

a. There is no distinction between citizens and allies in space allowance:
b. The cavalryman has four times the space of the infantryman (83.33 x 4 = 333.32)
c. The infantryman's space allowance in sq. feet (83.33) is 5/6ths of 100.

But while the blocks are marked out in feet, not *actus*; the tented area appears to have been planned in *actus quadrati* (*a.q.*) because the infantry have virtually 100 *a.q* and the cavalry about 50 *a.q*. See Table 2.3.

TABLE 2.3

TENT SPACE IN THE POLYBIAN CAMP

(One a.q. = 14400 sq. feet)

	Space per man	Total sq. feet	*a.q.*
16,800 infantry	83.33	1,399,944	97.22
2,400 cavalry	333.33	799,992	55.55
	totals	2,199,936	152.77

The precursor of the Polybian camp

This arrangement strongly suggests that the original infantry share was 100 *a.q.* to the cavalry's 50 *a.q.* If the combined area (150 *a.q.*) is multiplied by 6/5 it gives an area within the *intervallum* of 180 *a.q.* The *intervallum* would have been 201 feet: $[(\sqrt{180})/8] \times 120$. The Polybian camp therefore appears to have more cavalry and fewer infantry than the earlier model. The relevant features of the Polybian camp and its putative precursor are shown in Table 2.4.

TABLE 2.4

FEATURES OF THE POLYBIAN CAMP AND ITS PUTATIVE PREDECESSOR

(Areas in a.q.)

Areas	Pre-Polybian camp	Polybian camp	Change
Tented area of infantry	100	97.22	- 2.78
Tented area of cavalry	50	55.55	+5.55
Total tented area	150	152.77	+2.77
Area within intervallum	180	183.33	+3.33
Area of the intervallum	101	100.9	- 0.1
Area at the rampart	281	282.5	+ 1.5

The pre-Polybian consular army

These observations imply that the consular army of Polybius was a modification of an earlier model. The difference in infantry space (2.78 *a.q.*) accounts for 480 men, and that for cavalry (5.55 *a.q*) accounts for 240 men; a ratio of 2 to 1. The pre-Polybian army would therefore have numbered 17,280 infantry and 2,160 cavalry. If the infantry were split equally between citizens and allies, the legion numbered 4,320 men possibly organised in 36 maniples, each of two centuries of 60. Likewise, the cavalry could have comprised 72 *turmae*, each of 30 men. The likely partition of cavalry was 48 allied *turmae* (1,440 men) to 24 legionary (720 men). Thus the cavalry, each of whom had four times the infantryman's space, would have taken up half the area of the infantry because they were only one eighth of their numbers (17,280 / 8 = 2,160). This shows the sort of remodelling that had been going on during the third century BC, with the infantry becoming organised in units of 60 that were then combined into maniples of 120 and 180. The loss of 480 infantry made room for 120 cavalry but another 120 were added. See Table 2.5.

TABLE 2.5

CHANGES IN THE CONSULAR ARMY PRIOR TO THE POLYBIAN CAMP

	Pre Polybian army	Change	Polybian army
Infantry	17,280	480 men less	16,800
Cavalry	2,160	240 men more	2,400
Totals	19,440		19,200

Manpower for camp construction

The Polybian camp had a perimeter of 8,068 feet (4 x 2,017) which divided among the 16,800 infantry, gave 0.48 feet to each; exactly one tenth of the 4.8 feet per man seen with the basic model discussed in Chapter One. This is unlikely to be a co-incidence. If only half the infantry were assigned to the ditch and rampart, there was one foot of perimeter per man. This returns us to the question of manpower.

The various tasks involved in camp construction were performed with a division of labour. Writing in the first century AD, but doubtless referring to a long established practice, Josephus (3.71) tells us; "...nor do they tackle the job with *all their manpower* or without organised squads..." (Author's italics) There were three steps in making the camp: 1) site clearance, 2) marking-out the rectangle, 3) making the rampart and digging the ditch.

Site clearance
"...if the ground is uneven," wrote Josephus (3.71), "it is thoroughly levelled..." Modern military data suggest that one man could clear scrub at the rate of 33 sq. metres (355 sq. feet) per hour (Peddie 1996-7, 151). This is 0.025 *a.q.*, so the approximately 280 *a.q.* Polybian camp site would take 11,200 man hours (280 / 0.025) to prepare. If half the infantry (8,400) were put to the task, it would take them 1.33 hours (11,200 / 8,400).

Laying out the rectangle
The drill for setting-out the camp must have been speedy and accurate. Using the *groma* to set out axes of the desired length and fixing the perimeter with cross-sightings would not take long. If the lines were laid out at walking pace, say four feet per second, an *actus* could be paced in 30 seconds, or two per minute. If two axes were set out from the centre and the square defined at the inner margin of the *intervallum*, six lines of 13.42 *actus* would be needed. Each would take 13.42 x 30 seconds, or seven minutes. Six men working together could do it in less than ten minutes. These are only rough figures but are enough to show that a trained team could easily set out the square while site clearance was underway.

Rampart and ditch
The greatest labour was expended on the rampart and ditch but as we have seen, the paradigm had been established precisely with this in mind. The man-hours needed would depend on the nature of the ground. Using the argument set out in Chapter One, let us suppose a Roman soldier could manage to dig and shift 20 cu. feet of earth per hour. Each foot length of a V-section ditch, five feet wide and three feet deep, would account for 7.5 cu. feet of earth. So a perimeter of 8,068 feet would account for 60,645 cu. feet. The

man-hours needed to dig it would be 60,645 / 20 = 3,032. So with 8,400 men, the work could be done in 3,032 / 8,400 = 0.36 hours (22 minutes). This does not include making the rampart but if that task took three times as long, the perimeter was probably completed in under an hour and a half. There can be little doubt that the consular army at the time of the Punic Wars could make its camp defences in less than two hours with half its infantry, while the rest could pitch tents and fend off the enemy.

The Roman Army in Spain

There are no more explicit sources from the republic to inform us of the further development of the camp. The next evidence must be derived from the field works made at Renieblas, near Numantia in Spain, in the mid 2nd century BC.

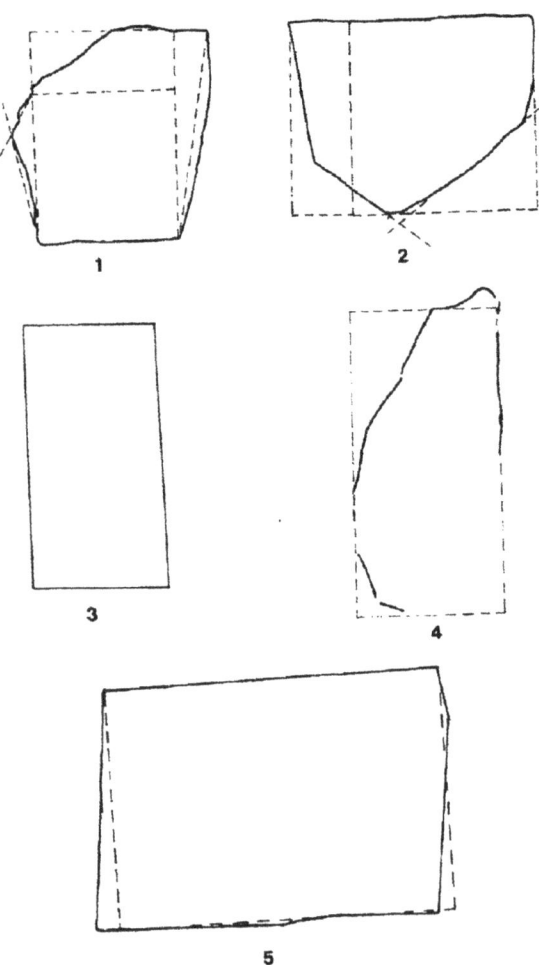

FIGURE 2.2: ROMAN CAMPS IN SPAIN: (NOT TO SCALE)

(After Keppie 1984: 1 = Renieblas III: 2 = Castillejo: 3 = Caceres: 4 = Pena Redonda: 5 = Renieblas V)

These camps were excavated by Schulten in the first decade of the 20th century and his plans, as re-published by Keppie (1984), were used for the studies reported here. There were five camps; camps I and II have fragmentary outlines from which the complete square, or rectangular, outline cannot be reconstructed. Camp III is roughly square but fits the contours of the hill upon which it stands in a way reminiscent of the Greek method mentioned by Polybius. Camps IV and V have oblong outlines with rounded corners like all subsequent examples.

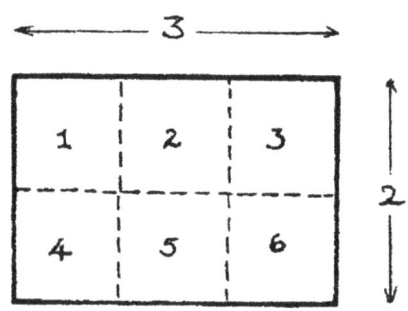

FIGURE 2.3

SUB-DIVISIONS OF A 2: 3 RECTANGLE

The oblong shape has a slightly longer perimeter than a square of the same area. The calculations needed after the adoption of the oblong will be dealt with in the next chapter but for the moment we must merely note that changing a given area from a square to an oblong with sides in the ratio of 2 to 3, the preferred option, increases the perimeter by only 2 %. A square of 100 *a.q.* has a sides of 10 *actus* and a perimeter of 40 (4 x 10) *actus*. A 2 by 3 oblong of the same area may be regarded as comprising six sub-squares arranged 2 by 3. See Figure 2.3. The area of each sub-square is 100/6 = 16.666 *a.q.* The side of each sub-square is √16.666, or 4.082. The perimeter is made up of ten such lengths; 40.825. The difference is 0.825 *actus* over 40, or 2.06 %. For all practical purposes the shape of a camp does not affect the area.

The *intervallum* at Numantia

The plans of these camps in Spain show internal buildings close to the rampart so the *intervallum* was less than a tenth of the sq. root the enclosed area. Since Renieblas III covered about 111 acres, or about 345 *a.q.* (111 x 3.215), its *intervallum* should have been 223 feet. The plan suggests it was about 90 feet, so the area within (A) was about 290 *a.q.* The *intervallum* at Renieblas V was about 50 feet and at Pena Redonda about 95 feet. Far from being 1/10th √R, they appear to be 1/24, 1/56 and 1/12 √R respectively. These are similar values to those found in legionary fortresses (see below) and suggest that the Numantian camps were more in the nature of permanent structures; perhaps because they were siege works.

Space allocations at Numantia

Schulten excavated a barrack block within Renieblas camp III and the space allocations to the men can be deduced from his plan. See Figure 2.4. The block measured approximately 672 x 460 feet and comprised 20 square sub-blocks, which seem originally to have been court-yards with buildings on three sides. Cavalry (five *turmae*) occupied five sub-blocks and the infantry the other 15. Five infantry sub-blocks lay adjacent to the cavalry, separated from the others by a roadway. According to Dr Keppie this barrack held half a legion; 15 infantry maniples of 160 men and five *turmae*. On this reckoning, there were 2,400 infantry and 150 cavalry in the barrack and 4,800 infantry and 300 cavalry to the legion.

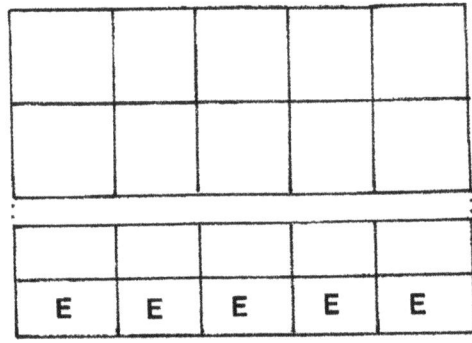

FIGURE 2.4: BARRACK AT RENIEBLAS III

(After Schulten (1933) and Keppie (1984): Sub-blocks marked "E" were for cavalry)

The dimensions and space allowances derived from the plan are shown in Table 2.6. While the cavalryman had virtually the same space as in the Polybian camp (336 sq. feet), the infantryman had about a third of this, not a quarter. Does this mean that he was now treated more generously, or were there more than 160 men to each sub-block? In view of the narrow *intervallum* the likely explanation is that the men had more space in this camp because it was more in the nature of a permanent fort.

TABLE 2.6

ESTIMATED SPACE ALLOWANCES AT RENIEBLAS CAMP III

(Presumes 2,400 infantry and 150 cavalry in the barrack)

Barrack dimensions	Feet	Area (sq. feet)	Area (*a.q.*)	Area per man (sq. feet)
Width of infantry part	672			
Depth of infantry part *	386	259,133	18.0	108
Width of cavalry part	672			
Depth of cavalry part	75	50,395	3.5	336
Total area			21.5	

* Includes the roadway.

The multiplier at Renieblas III

In the Polybian camp, the multiplier (m) of the tented area (T) to give the area (A) within the *intervallum* was 6/5. Was it the same in Spain 150 years later? We can approach the question by dividing the area within the *intervallum* (A) at Renieblas III by some likely values for m to find a range of values for T, the total barrack area. Then, if we divide these values by the area of one barrack block (21.5 *a.q.* See Table 2.6) we will find how many such barracks would fit within. The multiplier giving the nearest whole number value is likely to be the correct one. The area (A) was about 290 $a.q.$, see above, and the results of the calculations are shown in Table 2.7. Option three ($m = 1.333$ or $4/3$) is the most plausible because it gives virtually ten barrack blocks. These cover three-quarters of the area within the *intervallum* and suggest that the equivalent of five legions occupied the camp.

TABLE 2.7

OPTIONS FOR THE MULTIPLIER (m) AT RENIEBLAS III

m	Total barrack area	No of barracks
290 / 1.2	241.666	11.24
290 / 1.25	232.0	10.79
290 / 1.333	217.5	10.11

Other camps in Spain

The encampment at Pena Redonda has a coffin shaped outline, the *classica naval* (warship) of Hyginus (21), and Dr Keppie gives its area as 27 acres (about 84 $a.q.$). On his plan, the *intervallum* is about 80 feet, which is $1/12^{th}$ $\sqrt{R}$, and the area (A) is about 57 $a.q.$ Three quarters of this space is 42.75 $a.q.$; just right for two Renieblas III-type barrack blocks, which suggests the camp held one legion.

The *intervallum* at Castellejo, Numantia, is indefinable but its 18 acres within the ramparts is 2/3rds of the area of Pena Redonda, so it may have held 2/3rds of a legion. The later camp at Caceres, attributed by Schulten to Metellus Pius (about 80 BC) is twice the area of Pena Redonda (56 acres) and may have held the equivalent of two legions, rather than the one suspected.

The *intervallum* widths at Renieblas were not $1/10^{th}$ $\sqrt{R}$, but much narrower; indeed similar to those seen with permanent forts and fortresses. This raises two possibilities; that the *intervallum* was not determined by an inflexibly applied rule but chosen for convenience; or that these siege works, despite their temporary nature, were built according the rules for permanent structures. In this connection it may be significant that they were made of dry-stone walling and the space given to each infantryman was higher than in the Polybian camp. Considering these factors together with their irregular outlines and situation in hilly country, it is likely that the *intervallum* widths are atypical.

The evidence from Spain suggests that by the 140s BC, the legion had been re-modelled again and that by moving from a multiplier of 6/5 (1.2) to 4/3 (1.333) the proportion of space within the *intervallum* allocated to tent space was being diminished. This gave more room for roads, officers' tents, workshops and stores, without reducing the number of men per foot of perimeter and thus compromising its defence.

****

CHAPTER THREE

THE CAMP OF THE IMPERIAL ARMY

Camps of the imperial army

Most camps of the empire have vanished but the remains of a few have persisted, especially on unenclosed land. The most famous examples at Masada, Israel, have survived because like those at Numantia, they were part of siege works and made of dry-stone walling. More examples are known from aerial photography because their ditches have showed as crop-marks. All are rectangular with curved corners and the gates, which are simple breaks in the rampart, may be protected by deflections of the rampart (*claviculae*) either internal and encroaching on the *intervallum*, or external. Equally often, the gates are unprotected, or are furnished with a short straight section of bank and ditch (*titulus*) placed outside the gate. There is also a sub-set of gate types in Britain known from the reference site as Stracathro gates. Here a short, straight section of rampart points outwards on the side opposite a standard *clavicula*. The areas enclosed vary from under an acre to over 160 acres, obviously for forces varying from small units to great armies.

Camp outlines

These camps are often not square, like the Polybian camp, but oblong like those at Renieblas, and sometimes they have been further distorted from the orthogonal rectangle (right angles at each corner). These distortions may be slight, giving slightly "off square" outlines, or marked, resulting in parallelograms, trapezoids or asymmetrical shapes. The modifications were probably made to avoid unsuitable ground, such as bog or rocky ground, but Richmond (1962) believed they were due to the wind disturbing the plumb-bobs of the *groma* during the survey. At first sight this seems scarcely credible, since the plumb bobs were probably stabilised in buckets of water, but it may be true that the outline was also influenced by augury. But despite these features, it is usually possible to detect the rectangle upon which a camp was based, since the modifications were due to nothing more than rotating one or more of the ramparts about a fixed point on the perimeter of the base rectangle. See Figure 3.1.

Aspect ratio

The ratio of the length to breadth of an oblong is known as its *aspect ratio* and according to Hyginus (21) the preferred ratio was 2 by 3. He says this was for ventilation and to expedite the trumpet signals, but this cannot be the whole story. Indeed, the real reason takes us to into the realm of the quasi-reverence for numbers that seems to have been a feature of Roman military practice.

Aspect ratios were defined by a rule which ensured that the camp outlines fell between a 2:3 aspect ratio and a square. Hyginus (21) noted, "If it (the camp) is broader, the lay-out approaches a square." His word *approaches* is significant because, with few exceptions, camp rectangles have ratios in which the long axis is always one digit higher than the short axis; i.e., 2:3, 3:4, 4:5, 5:6, and so on. Algebraically, they conform to the rule $n : (n + 1)$ and if this progression continues, the aspect ratio *approaches* a square but, in purely mathematical terms, never reaches it. In practice, this was not important and is scarcely noticeable, but the rule kept the camp somewhere between the 2:3 ratio and the square. The ratio $n ; (n +1)$ was known in Pythagoras's time as the *harmonic* mean, as distinct from the *arithmetic* and *geometric* mean, and it was re-defined by Archytas of Taras about 400 BC (Heath 1921, 84-90).

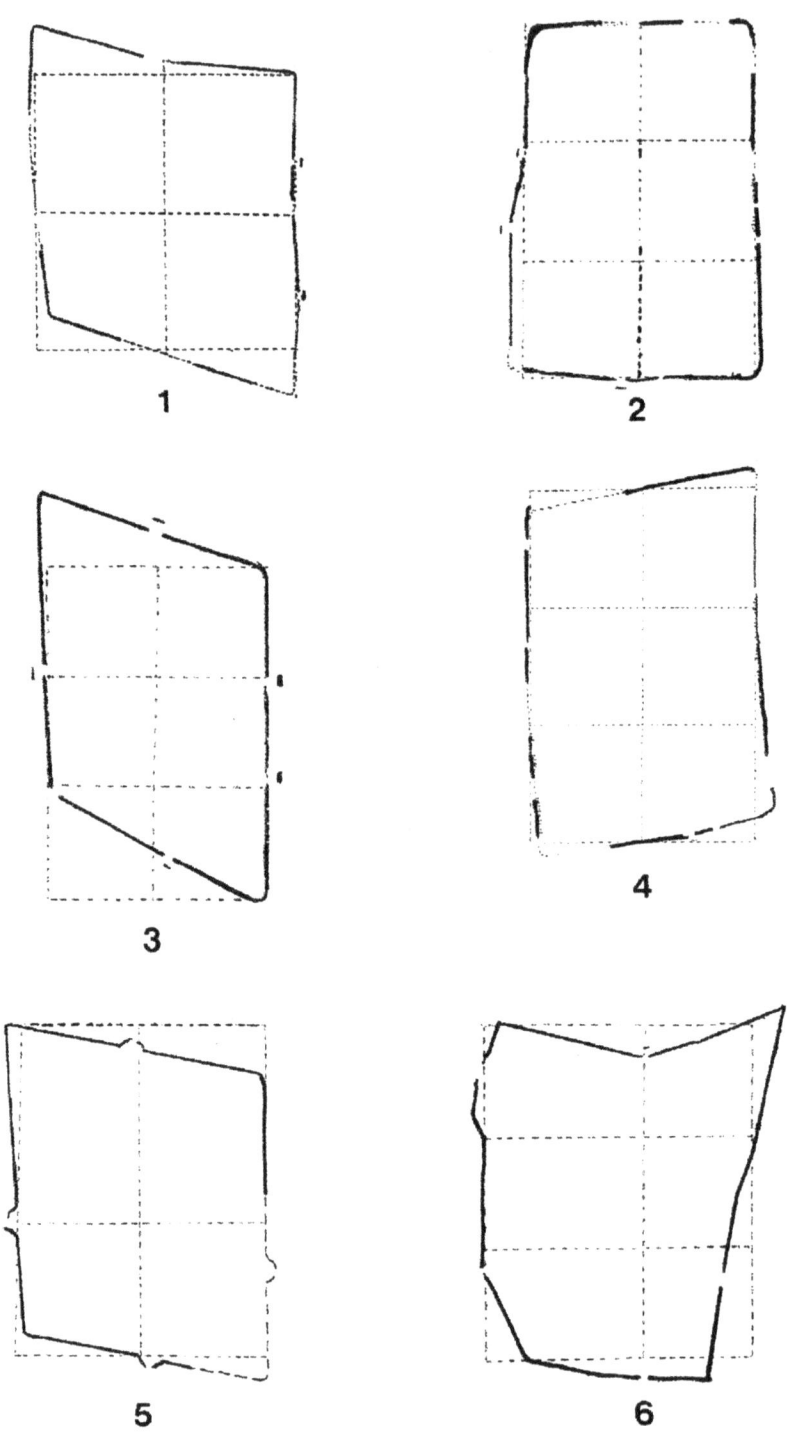

FIGURE 3.1: OBLONG ROMAN CAMPS: NOT TO SCALE

(1 Abernethy, square: 2 Ardoch 4, 2 by 3: 3 Featherwood West, 2 by 3: 4 Ardoch 6, 2 by 3: 5 Stracathro, 4 by 5: 6 Rae Dykes, 5 by 6)

There is no doubt that for the followers of Pythagoras, mathematical quirks had a religious significance that is difficult for us to grasp. The square is a familiar and geometrically simple shape to deal with, and we have seen how it fitted with the numerical structure of the army; but why the 2:3 ratio? The answer is probably because it was the nearest harmonic mean to the "golden section", a proportion that was imbued with mystical significance for the ancients on account of its aesthetic properties which were invoked in both art and architecture. It is best imagined as a line so divided that the ratio of the short section to the long is the same as the long section to the whole. It is not a finite number for it has a never-ending sequence after the decimal point, like Pi (π). Expressed to the third decimal place, it is 0.618 whereas the fraction 2/3 is 0.666. *

Occasionally, the aspect ratio did not follow the n : (n + 1) rule and the long axis was disproportionately long. In this case the camp was called a "warship" (*classica naval*). In a sample of 93 camps, the aspect ratios were distributed as shown in Table 3.1. The 2:3 ratio was the commonest, followed by the 4:5 ratio, though almost exactly half as frequent. The three cited examples (3 %) are of the *classica naval*.

TABLE 3.1

FREQUENCY OF ASPECT RATIOS OF ROMAN CAMPS

(After Richardson 2001)

Aspect ratio	% of sample	Examples	Aspect ratio	% of sample
1:1 (square)	14		7:8	4
1:2	6		8:9	1
1:3	1	Cawthorn C	9:10	1
2:3	29		10:11	5
3:4	3		11:12	0
3:5	1	Uffington 2	12:13	0
3:8	1	Sills Burn S	13:14	1
4:5	15		14:15	0
5:6	10		15:16	1
6:7	4		16:17	0

Calculating the dimensions of an oblong camp

Each axis (or side) of a square camp is the sq. root of the area but special formulae were needed to calculate the lengths of the axes of the oblong camp. They remain unknown but it is possible to suggest two which may have been used. Consider a rectangle with an aspect ratio n : (n + 1). It can be divided into a number of sub-squares. See Figure 3.2.

---

* The mean of any two numbers in the n : (n + 1) series cannot be a whole number and for some reason Greek mathematicians thought this property was special. See Heath (1921).

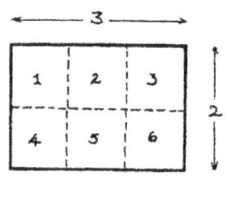

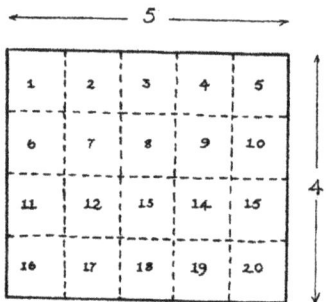

FIGURE 3.2: SUB-SQUARES IN OBLONGS WITH ASPECT RATIOS OF N : N + 1

If the long axis is the *decumanus* (d) and the short axis is the *cardo* (c) the aspect ratio is c : d. The number of sub-squares is c times d; written c d. If the area of the rectangle is A, then the area of each sub-square is A / c d. The side of a sub-square is $\sqrt{A/cd}$. Therefore the length of the short axis is $c\sqrt{(A/cd)}$ and the long axis is $d\sqrt{(A/cd)}$. Algebraically, we have

$$D = d\sqrt{(A/cd)}. \quad \text{and} \quad C = c\sqrt{(A/cd)}$$

Where D = *decumanus* in *actus*; C = *cardo* in *actus*; A = area in *a.q.* and c : d is the desired aspect ratio.

Take the 180 *a.q.* area within the *intervallum* of the pre-Polybian camp. The length of the side of the square camp is √180, or 13.41 *actus*. Suppose we wish to convert it to a 2:3 ratio. To find the lengths of the long axis we apply the formula, thus:

$D = 3\sqrt{(180 / 2 \times 3)}$

$D = 3\sqrt{(180 / 6)}$

$D = 3\sqrt{30}$

$D = 3 \times 5.45$

$D = 16.43$ *actus*

The calculation for the cardo (C) gives 10.95 *actus*, so the area is 16.43 x 10.95 = 180 *a.q.*

De munitionibus castrorum

There is not a published English translation of this work so the author used a manuscript translation made by Sir Ian Richmond for W. G. Simpson in 1925 and kindly lent by Dr Grace Simpson. It is now in the Sackler Library, Oxford, and is reproduced in Appendix One. Hyginus appears to have been commissioned to search the literature and explain to his master how to make a camp. Though he admitted he could not find the underlying principles of laying-out the rectangle, he reported a great deal of detail about the units and the space they required. The army had changed since the days of Polybius; new units had come into existence and the tents were now pitched back-to-back in rows 60 feet (0.5 *actus*) wide and known as *strigae*. Each tent row, and the space in front, occupied a depth of 30 feet, the *hemistrigium*, whose symmetry had to be preserved. Hyginus gives the space allocated to each unit as the number of feet along the *hemistrigium*, revealing that each one normally occupied a certain number of *actus*. Dividing that length by four gives the number of *a.q.* occupied by the unit, because the *hemistrigium* was ¼ *actus* deep.

The imperial army

The army in the Hyginian camp is that of the empire, a fully professional force which, while retaining the legions (citizens), replaced the allies with regular, non-citizen auxiliaries organised in cohorts. These were quingenary (nominally 500 strong) or milliary (nominally 1,000 strong) but actually comprising numbers that are the nearest multiples of 60 or 80. The cavalry *turmae* were further combined into *alae*; again normally quingenary and milliary, but actually based on multiples of eight; *viz.* 16 and 24. There were also combined infantry and cavalry units, *cohortes equitatae*, both quingenary and milliary, and the emperor, when present, was attended by a contingent of praetorian troops whose infantry were given twice the normal infantry space. Table 3.2 lists the units of this organisation.

TABLE 3.2

ORGANISATION OF THE IMPERIAL ARMY

(After Breeze & Dobson 2000)

	Quingenaria	Milliaria
Legionary	cohortes II – X	cohors I
Auxiliary infantry	cohors peditata quingenaria	cohors peditata milliaria
Auxiliary cavalry	ala quingenaria	ala milliaria
Mixed auxiliary units	cohors equitata quingenaria	cohors equitata milliaria

Table 3.3 shows the composition of these units. The figures in brackets, for which there is some evidence, probably represent modifications made under particular circumstances.

TABLE 3.3

COMPOSITION OF UNITS IN THE IMPERIAL ARMY

(After Breeze & Dobson 2000)

Unit	Infantry Centuries	Men/Century	Cavalry Turmae	Men / Turma	Total in unit
Legionary					
cohors I	5 double	160	-	-	800
cohors II - X	6	80	-	-	480
Equites legionis	-	-	4 ?	30 ?	120
Auxiliary					
cohors ped. quin.	6	80 (100)	-	-	480 (600)
cohors ped. mill.	10	80 (100)	-	-	800 (100)
ala quingenaria.	-	-	16	30 (32)	480 (512)
ala milliaria.	-	-	24	30 (32) (42)	720 (768) (1008)
cohors equ. quin.	6	80 (60)	4	30 (32)	600 (608)
cohors equ. mill.	10	80	8	30 (32)	1,040 (1056)

Tent space in the Hyginian camp

Each infantryman in the legions, and in those auxiliary units without cavalry, had 45 sq. feet of tent space compared to 83.33 sq. feet in the Polybian camp; a 54 % reduction. The cavalry in the *alae* had 90 sq. feet, or twice that of the infantryman, not four times; a 27 % reduction. A cohort of legionaries (480 men) therefore occupied 1.5 *a.q.* of *strigae*, while a *turma* took up 0.1875 (3/16ths) *a.q.* This was 1/8th of the space given to an infantry cohort. In the mixed auxiliary units, *cohortes equitatae*, the men had slightly less space, each infantryman having 36 sq. feet and each cavalryman having 81 sq. feet, though it is possible that originally these cavalry had twice the space of the infantry, *viz.* 72 sq. feet.

These changes undoubtedly reflect the increased professionalism of the imperial army. Men and horses packed into small spaces must be especially well-trained and organised and compared with the camp of the republic, everything is tightened up. There are more men per unit of area, so the effect was to increase greatly the numbers available to make and man the defences. This meant that more time, and more men, were available to take an active role in patrolling, foraging and engaging the enemy. There can be no doubt that these changes greatly enhanced the army's effectiveness.

Notional cohorts

It is now necessary, to consider an aspect of Roman military planning for which there is no direct testimony but for which there is much indirect evidence; namely, a planning unit that enabled different cavalry and infantry combinations to be handled simply when calculating camp areas.

The areas of *strigae* allotted to the different units are shown in Table 3.4. The last column gives the unit's area of *strigae* relative to that of an infantry cohort; that is, its strigified area divided by 1.5.

TABLE 3.4

SPACE ALLOWANCES IN CAMPS DERIVED FROM HYGINUS

Unit	Hemistrigium (feet)	Hemistrigium (actus)	Strigae (actus)	Strigae (area of) (a.q.)	Infantry cohort-equivalent
Infantry century	120	1.0	0.5	0.25	-
Infantry cohort	720	6.0	3.0	1.5	1.0
Ala quingenaria (480)	14,400	12.0	6.0	3.0	2.0
(512)	1356	12.8	6.4	3.2	2.13
Ala milliaria (720)	2160	18.0	9.0	4.5	3.0
(768)	2304	19.2	9.6	4.8	3.2
(1008)	3024	25.2	12.6	6.3	4.2
Cohors equitatae quin.	900	7.5	3.75	1.875	1.25
Cohors equitatae mill.	1608	13.4	6.7	3.35	2.23

Because the cavalryman now had twice the space of the infantryman, in space terms 60 infantry = 30 cavalry. A cohort of 480 infantry therefore needed the space of 240 cavalry and the *ala quingenaria* (480 cavalry) needed the space of two infantry cohorts. The exceptions to the rule were the praetorian infantry which had twice the space of ordinary infantry and therefore counted as cavalry.

It follows that all units, in terms of space requirement, may be regarded as multiples of an infantry cohort. See Table 3.4, column 6, headed infantry cohort-equivalent. The author has suggested the term *notional cohort* for this value. A legionary cohort rates as one; an *ala quingenaria* as two and an *ala milliaria* with 720 men rates as three. Another way of expressing the notional cohort value of a unit would be (number of infantry / 480) and (number of cavalry / 240) but for the praetorian infantry rating as cavalry and the *cohortes equitatae* having a reduced space allowances (Table 3.4). The first legionary cohort in the imperial legion, like the *cohors milliaria peditata*, comprised 800 men and rates as 800/480 = 1.666 notional cohorts.

The army therefore came to be organised into units that were themselves multiples of 60 infantry (*centuriae*) and 30 cavalry (*turmae*) that occupied the same space. An infantry cohort was 480 (60 x 8), though often it may have been managed as six centuries of 80. There is also evidence of quingenary infantry cohorts with six centuries of 100 men. Such units had a notional cohort number of 1.25 and can be detected in certain forts (see Chapter Four). Table 3.5 lists the units and their notional cohort values. Note that the multiples are simple fractions.

TABLE 3.5

TACTICAL UNITS AS MULTIPLES OF ONE NOTIONAL COHORT

Unit	Multiples	Men	Centuries	Turmae
Infantry				
Leg. cohors I	480 x 1.666	800	5 double	-
Leg. cohors II -X	480 x 1	480	6	-
cohors ped. quin.	480 x 1	480	6	-
cohors ped.(600)	480 x 1.25	600	6 (80 men)	-
cohors ped. mill.	480 x 1.666	800	10	-
Cavalry				
Equites legionis	240 x 0.5	120	-	4
ala quin.	240 x 2	480	-	16
ala mill.	240 x 3	720	-	24
"	240 x 4.2	1,008	-	24 (42 men)
Mixed units				
cohors equ. quin.	(480 x 1) + (240 x 0.5)		6 (80 men)	4
cohors equ. mill.	(480 x 1.666) + (240 x 0.5)		10 (80 men)	4

The notional cohort concept thus enables infantry and cavalry to be treated as common currency with regard to space within the camp and it is likely that Romans used some similar term in their planning. The legion comprised a milliary first cohort (1.666) and nine quingenary cohorts, rated at one each (9 x 1), giving a total of 10.666. To this were added the legionary cavalry rated at 0.5 (120/240), giving a total of 11.166. This is an awkward number so it was probably rounded up to 12.

The Multiplier in the Hyginian camp

Hyginus implies he is describing a camp that was 12 by 18 *actus* or 216 *a.q.* in area. Curiously, this is ten times the size of a barrack block at Renieblas III. The camp was for three legions with auxiliaries, all of which he listed. From his space allowance data it is possible to calculate the areas of *strigae* and the number of notional cohorts in the whole force, though the results depend upon how certain ambiguities are handled. For example, did the cavalry in the *cohortes equitatae* have 81 sq. feet each as Hyginus suggests, or the 72 sq. feet as might be supposed from the rule in the non-mixed units? Similarly, did the *ala milliaria* have 720, 768 or 1,008 cavalry?

The numbers of these troops, their areas of *strigae* and the computed numbers of notional cohorts are shown in Table 3.6. This model assumed that:

a) The *cohortes equitatae* had the reduced area allowance;
b) The *ala milliaria* had 720 men;
c) The legions occupied the *strigae* strictly according to the space allowances per man, rather than according to a notional cohort number of 12;
d) All tribal units were cavalry.

TABLE 3.6

TROOP NUMBERS, STRIGAE AND NOTIONAL COHORTS IN THE HYGINIAN CAMP

(Strigae in a.q.: N = notional cohorts, i.e., Strigae / 1.5)

Military units Type	Number	Infantry Men	Strigae	Cavalry Men	Strigae	N
Legions	3	15,360	48.0	-	-	32.0
Vexillarii	-	1,600	5.0	-	-	3.33
Misenum fleet (marines)	-	500	1.6	-	-	1.0
Ravenna fleet (marines)	-	800	2.5	-	-	1.66
Cohortes mill. peditatae.	3	2,400	7.5	-	-	5.0
Cohortes quin. peditatae	3	14,400	4.5	-	-	3.0
Cohortes Praetoriae	4	1,920	12.0	-	-	8.0
Statores	-	160	0.5	-	-	0.3
Legionary cavalry	-	-	-	360	2.25	1.5
Alae quingenariae	5	-	-	2,400	15.0	10.0
Alae milliariae	4	-	-	2,880	18.0	12.0
Praetorian cavalry	-	-	-	400	2.5	1.66
Scouts	-	-	-	200	1.25	0.8
Praet. Cavalry (singulares)	-	-	-	450	2.81	1.9
Palmyrenes	-	-	-	500	33.1	2.0
Gaeticulae	-	-	-	900	5.63	3.75
Brittones	-	-	-	500	3.13	2.08
Cantabri	-	-	-	700	4.38	2.92
Mauritanians	-	-	-	600	3.75	2.5
Pannonians	-	-	-	800	5.0	3.33
Cohortes equitatae mill.	2	1,600	4.0	480	2.7	4.5
Cohortes equitatae quin.	4	1,920	4.8	480	2.7	5.0
Totals		27,700	90.36	11,650	77.21	108.4
Total men	39,350					
Total strigae	162.6					
Total notional cohorts	108.4					

In whole numbers, the total strigified area was 162 *a.q.* This is ¾ of 216 so the multiplier was 4/3 (1.333) as at Renieblas III. The area within the *intervallum* was thus one third bigger than the strigified area, with plenty of room for roadways, officers' tents, workshops and storage.

Since each notional cohort had 1.5 *a.q.* of *strigae*, it accounted for 1.5 x 4/3 or 2 *a.q.* within the *intervallum*. Thus, to know the area (A) in *a.q.* for an intended camp, the *praefectus castrorum* could merely double the number of notional cohorts. All he needed was the notional cohort number of each type of unit (soon memorised) and the number to be accommodated. For example, five *alae quingenariae* and ten *cohortes peditatae quingenariae* would total (5 x 2) + (10 x 1) = 20 notional cohorts. These would require a camp of 40 *a.q.* at the inner margin of the *intervallum*. The 108 notional cohorts listed in Table 3.6 needed 216 *a.q.*, or 12 x 18 *actus* within the *intervallum*.

This model fits perfectly, but in Table 3.6 the notional cohort value for each legion was made up as 10.666 infantry and 0.5 cavalry, giving a total of 11.16. When this figure is amended to 12, the total for the

Hyginian army becomes 110.9 and the area within the *intervallum* becomes 222 *a.q.* so the sides must become 12.16 and 18.35 *actus*.

The *intervallum* of the Hyginian camp

Hyginus reported an *intervallum* of only 60 feet for a camp for some 40,000 men and 15,000 horses. Given that it was for manoeuvre behind the rampart and to protect against missiles thrown over it, this is not believable. Other evidence has suggested Hyginus's error; in the Polybian camp the *intervallum* was $1/8^{th}\sqrt{A}$ and at Masada B, where the *intervallum* was often uneven, a mathematical analysis strongly suggested that it was the same (Richardson 2000). The dimensions of 12 x 18 *actus* gives a rectangle of 216 a.q. so the *intervallum* should have been $(\sqrt{216})/8$, or 1.83 *actus* (220 feet); a far more realistic width than 60 feet.

Acreage of imperial army camps

Because the model is linear the number of notional cohorts correlates closely with the camp's area at the inner face of the rampart. The actual correlation in terms of acreage is, *notional cohorts* (N) = *acres* / 0.981. The Hyginian camp would have been 337 *a.q.* (108 acres) at the rampart since one *a.q.* is 0.3215 acres. There are in Scotland at least three similar camps; Normandykes (106 acres); Muiryfold (109 acres) and Kintore (110 acres).

The emperor's contingent

TABLE 3.7

UNITS ATTACHED TO THE EMPEROR IN THE HYGINIAN CAMP

Units	Men	Strigae (a.q.)	Notional cohorts
Infantry			
Vexillarii	1,600	5.0	3.33
Misenum fleet	500	1.6	1.0
Ravenna fleet	800	2.5	1.66
Praetorian cohorts	1,920	12.0	8.0
Statores	160	0.5	0.33
	4,980		
Cavalry			
Praetorian cavalry	400	2.5	1.66
Equitates Sing. Imp.	450	2.8	1.86
	850		
Totals	5,830	26.9	17.9 (18)

Table 3.7 shows the space allocations of those troops attached to the emperor but not part of the normal field army; *vexillarii*, marines, praetorians and *statores*. These required 26.9 (say 27) *a.q.* of *strigae*,

enough for 18 notional cohorts that would add 36 *a.q.* to the area within the *intervallum* and increase the area at the rampart by 56.2 *a.q.* (18 acres). Hyginus (10) writes that the emperor's court had from 50 to 70 feet of *hemistrigium*. This is only 0.15 *a.q.* across the *strigium*, or the space given to a tenth of cohort (48 men). This seems somewhat modest, given the ostentation of the emperor's lifestyle, but perhaps he was prepared to rough it when on campaign. If he and his personal staff required the space of a cohort, they would increase the area by only one acre.

Summary of the imperial army camp paradigm

The paradigm for the Hyginian camp may be summarised thus:

1. N = notional cohort number
2. S (*strigae* in *a.q.*) = $N \times 1.5$
3. A (area within the *intervallum*) = $S \times 1.333$, or $A = N \times 2$
4. $I = (\sqrt{A}) / 8$.
5. The area at the inner face of the rampart (R) is $(\sqrt{A} + 2I)^2$

These equations can be used in a computer spreadsheet to model camps for any combination of imperial army units. A spreadsheet is like a chess board into whose squares separate bits of information, or mathematical formulae, may be inserted. Each square is identified by a reference code, so, for example, into one square (cell) can be inserted an instruction (formula) to manipulate values in other cells. The formulae may be complex and several mathematical processes besides addition and subtraction can be carried out. The cells may be linked together in a chain so that when one value is changed, the whole chain is re-calculated. It is a very rapid way of asking "what if" questions and ideal for calculating rapidly the areas and dimensions of camps. Table 3.8 illustrates the main features of camps for a legion (12 notional cohorts) and for a vexilation of half a legion (6 notional cohorts).

TABLE 3.8

FEATURES OF LEGIONARY CAMPS

(Areas in a.q.)

	One legion	Half a legion
N = notional cohorts	12	6
S (strigae) = N x 1.5	18	9
A = S x 1.333, or N x 2	24	12
I = Intervallum ($\sqrt{A}$) / 8	0.61 actus, or 74 feet	0.43 actus, or 52 feet.
A = ($\sqrt{A}$ = 2I) squared	37.44	18.7
Possible examples	Burnswalk Sth *	Chew Green 4
	Kirkby Thore 1	Cawthorn B
	Wath	Broomby Lane 1

* Keppie (1984): all other camps from Welfare & Swan (1995)

The partition of space within the camp

It is, of course, an open question as to whether this paradigm was applied rigidly in all circumstances. When large numbers of prisoners, livestock and booty were captured, the camp area may have been increased over and above that dictated by the paradigm, but if so, there were implications for the labour available for the defences. The question is particularly relevant to the large camps in Scotland which will be discussed below. On the other hand, there are good grounds for believing that the paradigm allowed for accommodating prisoners and storing booty in most situations. Table 3.9 shows the partition of space within the camp. Over a third of the area within the rampart was *intervallum* and although its prime function was for organising defence and traffic, a certain amount must have been available as storage space.

TABLE 3.9

PARTITION OF SPACE WITHIN THE CAMP

(After Richardson 2003: R = area within the rampart; A = area within the *intervallum*)

Area	% R	% A
Within the *intervallum* (A)	64	-
Of the *Intervallum*	36	56
Strigae (men's' tents)	48	75
Praetorium, Roads, etc	16	25

The siting and orientation of camps

The choice of camp site was obviously important. The factors that had to be to considered fall under three headings; the position in relation to the enemy: the ground conditions and orientation with respect to the points of the compass. The final decision must have reflected a compromise between conflicting imperatives.

The ideal site was a gentle slope facing the enemy, not overlooked by nearby hills and with access to drinking water. Hyginus (56) reported that the situations were graded. "So far as the choice of ground in determining the layout is concerned," he wrote, "that position is considered first class which rises gently to a height from the plain: in such a position the *Porta Decumana* is fixed at the highest point, so that the different parts of the camp may lie beneath it. The *Porta Praetoria* should always face the enemy. The position considered second class is level; third class on a hill; fourth class on a mountain; fifth class in an unavoidable position - whence the term 'necessary camp'." (Richmond 1925). "But," added Vegetius (1.23) "the gate which is called *praetoria* should either face east, or the direction which looks towards the enemy, or if on the march it should face the direction in which the army is to proceed." (Milner 1993, 24).

Vegetius implies that the alignment should be EW only if the enemy were not nearby. Milner (1993, 24) suggested this was perhaps in deference to Christianity since, Vegetius wrote after the establishment of that religion in the empire. The only other interpretation is that the Roman force was always to place itself west of the enemy position, which is not credible. On the other hand, Dilke (1971, 56, 86) has stated,

"Many *agrimensores* started as military surveyors and for camp sites an orientation by the compass points was customary" and "When no considerations of terrain arise, Roman camps tend to be orientated towards the four points of the compass." He did not cite any supporting reference for either of these statements but presumably had come across them in his study of the *Corpus Agrimensorum*. It is clear that the orientation was an important matter and that the final choice reflected a compromise between conflicting imperatives.

****

CHAPTER FOUR

FORTS, FORTLETS AND LEGIONARY FORTRESSES

The fort paradigm

The fort was conceptually the same as the camp; an outer rectangle defining the inner face of the rampart (R) within which the *intervallum* (I) surrounded an inner rectangle (A) that contained the buildings. Outside the rampart were one or more ditches. Though forts were usually made of turf and timber with wooden buildings, some were of stone and lasted until the end of the Roman period.

The fort *intervallum* was typically $1/18^{th}$ of the square root of the area at the inner face of the rampart (R) and $1/16^{th}$ of the square root of the area within the *intervallum* (A) but there was some variation. The same rule for aspect ratios was applied but later re-building of ramparts has altered the outlines of many forts. Moreover, because some later housed other types of unit, the correlation between area and unit is not always clear.

Instead of each notional cohort being given 2 *a.q.* within the *intervallum*, the space allowance varied between 6 and 8 *a.q.* and henceforth, when the term "space allowance" is used in relation to forts, it shall mean with respect to one notional cohort.

The notional cohort number of a unit for which the fort was intended can be found by dividing the area (A) by putative space allowances between 6 and 8 *a.q.* This usually gives at least one recognisable notional cohort number, which may be regarded as the unit's "signature". Often a space allowance of 8 *a.q.* for one type of unit fits the next biggest unit at 6 *a.q.* For example, a fort with 10 *a.q.* within its *intervallum* fits 1.25 notional cohorts (*cohors peditata quingenaria* with 600 men) at a space allowance of 8 *a.q.* (10 / 8 = 1.25). But, because 10 / 6 = 1.666 notional cohorts, a *cohors peditata milliaria* can be accommodated at 6 *a.q.* The men in *cohortes equitatae*, who were allowed slightly less space than the other units in the temporary camp, appear to have been treated equally when in permanent quarters; the evidence derives from a signature of 1.5 (*cohors quingenaria equitata*) that can be found at several forts.

A spreadsheet for finding notional cohort signatures may start with the dimensions of the fort at the inner face of the rampart, which should be carefully measured from the plan. The equations are:

1. Length x width at the inner rampart (*actus*) = R *a.q.*
2. The *intervallum* (I) = $(\sqrt{R}) / 18$.
3. The area within the *intervallum* (A) = $[(\sqrt{R}) - 2I]^2$
4. The notional cohort number (N) = A / 8, or A / 7 or A / 6.

Fendoch

This exercise usually gives plausible results but sometimes these may conflict with an existing interpretation of the site. In such cases the evidence from the site must overrule any interpretation based on the paradigm alone, but not without a critical inquiry. The fort at Fendoch, Perthshire, provides a good example. The plan published by Collingwood & Richmond (1969, 30) shows a fort with a 1:2 aspect ratio. The inner margin of the *intervallum* defines a regular (right angles at each corner) oblong, 510 by 255 feet, or 9.0 *a.q.* An *intervallum* of $1/16^{th}$ $\sqrt{A}$ would be 22.5 feet wide. The Fendoch *intervallum*, however, is irregular so the fort outline tapers to one end. The mean width is about 27 feet, but a mean difference of 4.5 feet on a plan in a text book is negligible. Dividing the area (A), 9.0 *a.q.*, by space allowances (8, 7, and 6) gives notional cohort values of 1.125, 1.28 and 1.5, suggesting three possibilities:

1. A *cohors quingenaria peditata* (N = 1).
2. A 600-man unit infantry cohort (N = 1.25).
3. A *cohors quingenaria equitata* (N = 1.5).

But the closest agreement between the estimates and the putative signatures is option 3.

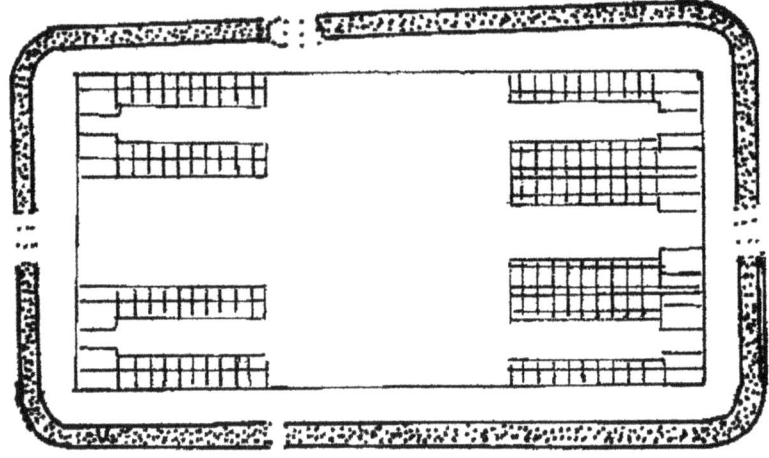

FIGURE 4.1:

BARRACKS AT FENDOCH FORT

(After Collingwood & Richmond 1969: Note the *intervallum* is asymmetrical, but the area within is a regular oblong.)

Collingwood and Richmond noted ten barrack blocks, each with ten rooms, and concluded that with eight men to a room, the fort held a *cohors milliaria peditata*. This unit comprises 1.666 notional cohorts and would fit Fendoch only with a space allowance of 5.4 *a.q.* (9.08 / 1.666). This is possible, but unlikely.

Unfortunately, Collingwood and Richmond's description of the barracks is not strictly accurate. In the *praetentura* (right of the *principia* in Figure 4.1) are four barracks, each with a two rows of 10 rooms (12 x 32 feet) giving a total of 80 rooms. The officers' rooms at each end are not counted. In the *retentura* there are 60 similarly sized rooms arranged in six rows of ten. But each of these is divided into two unequal parts. So, while there are ten barrack blocks, there are 140 rooms. But Collingwood and Richmond counted ten blocks and presumed a total of 100 rooms. Then, by allowing eight men to a room, they arrived at the figure of 800 men; the strength of a *cohors peditata milliaria*. The subdivisions within the rooms in the *retentura* were not taken into account. Moreover, had they postulated six men to a room, they would have seen evidence of a quingenary infantry cohort with 600 men (N = 1.25).

Considering these inconsistencies in the light of a probable notional cohort signature of a *cohors quingenaria equitata*, another interpretation can be offered. The numbers of men to a room and whether or not some rooms housed cavalrymen with their horses cannot be known, but some possibilities are set out in Table 4.1. The 80 rooms of the *praetentura* could hold the infantry component of a *cohors quingenaria equitata* (480) with six men to a room. The 60 rooms in the *retentura* could hold 120 "men" with two per room, but if these were cavalrymen with horses sharing their accommodation, the space is just right for the cavalry component of such a unit. In this situation, the infantry would have one third the space of the cavalry, as at Renieblas III, rather than twice as in the Hyginian camp.

TABLE 4.1

POSSIBLE TROOP NUMBERS AT FENDOCH

	No of rooms	No of men per room	
		2	6
praetentura	80	160	**480**
retentura	60	**120**	600

This interpretation discounts the horses being stabled separately, which is quite possible because there was no consistency about horse accommodation in forts (Johnson 1983, 176-182). Although they were sometimes kept in long stables, like cows in a byre, equally often they were kept in smaller rooms. There is no doubt that such an arrangement is healthier for both man and beast and therefore more desirable. Skin and respiratory diseases are a constant nuisance with group-stabled horses and it may be that various husbandry systems were tried during the early empire when permanent cavalry establishments became a feature of the Roman army.

Classifying forts according to unit

The author first tried to classify auxiliary forts on the supposition they were designed with a space allocation of 8 *a.q.*, with the capability of admitting larger units with smaller space allowances (Richardson 2000). This seemed to fit with the existence of five types of auxiliary unit (other then the *ala milliaria*). Data from more forts, however, has revealed that the areas tend to form a continuous series rather than fitting into discrete categories. Those at the lower end of the range merge into fortlets, while those at the upper end merge with forts for several units and legionary vexilations. But this continuum might be an artefact due to scale errors in the published plans blurring small dimensional differences between discrete groups.

Below are set out some examples of forts classified according to the type of unit that they seem to cater for. The selection is not a complete inventory from the literature. The area R was determined from the published plans and the value for (A) calculated on the basis of an *intervallum* of $1/18^{th}$ $\sqrt{R}$. The values reported are as derived from the plans and must admit of some small error. Probable notional cohort signatures are shown in bold type. This data set reveals that all but group one forts (mean 2.5 acres) were designed to fit two, or even three, types of unit.

GROUP ONE

Forts for *cohortes quingenariae peditatae*: (N =1).

Fort	R	N at given space allowances			Data source
		8 a.q	7 a.q.	6 a.q.	
Brough on Noe	7.2	0.7	0.8	0.85	Jones (1968)
Wall	7.3	0.7	0.8	0.95	Welfare & Swan (1995)
Whitley Castle	7.6	0.7	0.8	**1.0**	Collingwood & Richmond (1969)
Caerau A 1	7.8	0.8	0.9	**1.0**	St Joseph (1969)
Ambleside	7.9	0.8	0.9	**1.0**	Johnson (1983)
Ilkley 1	7.9	0.8	0.9	**1.0**	Hartley (1987)
Brough (St'more	8.0	0.8	0.9	**1.0**	Birley (1958)
Strageath (Fla)	8.2	0.8	0.9	**1.0**	Frere *et al* (1977)
Hayton (York)	8.3	0.8	0.9	**1.0**	Johnson (1978)
Old Penrith	8.3	0.8	0.9	**1.0**	Poulter (1982)
Bury Barton	8.8	0.9	**1.0**	1.1	Todd (1985)
Brampton Ch.	9.3	0.9	**1.0**	1.2	Robinson (1982)
Gelligaer	9.3	0.9	**1.0**	1.2	Collingwood & Richmond (1969)
Mean area	8.1 a.q. (2.5 acres)				

GROUP TWO

Forts for *cohortes quingenariae peditatae*: (N = 1) and 600-man infantry cohorts (N = 1.25)

Fort	R	N at given space allowances			Data source
		8 a.q	7 a.q.	6 a.q.	
Ilkley 2 & 3	9.5	0.9	**1.0**	**1.25**	Hartley (1987)
Elginhaugh (Fl)	9.6	0.9	**1.0**	**1.25**	Frere (1987)
Troutbeck 1	9.9	**1.0**	1.1	1.3	Welfare & Swan (1995)
Valkenburg	10	**1.0**	1.1	1.3	Johnson (1983)
Watercrook	10.2	**1.0**	1.1	1.3	Birley (1957)
Barochan Hill	10.4	**1.0**	1.1	1.4	Frere *et al* (1985)
Oberstimm	10.4	**1.0**	1.2	1.4	Johnson (1983)
Castle Shaw	10.5	**1.0**	1.2	1.4	Start (1985)
Melandra 1	10.5	**1.0**	1.2	1.4	Jones (1968)
Cawthorn D	10.7	**1.0**	1.2	1.4	Welfare & Swan (1995)
Stretford Bridge	10.8	**1.0**	1.2	1.4	Welfare & Swan (1995)
Drumquassle	10.9	**1.0**	1.2	1.4	Maxwell (1983)
Mean area	10.3 (3.3 acres)				

GROUP THREE

Forts for *cohortes quingenariae equitatae*: (N = 1.5) but capable of taking *cohortes quingenariae peditatae* (N = 1) including 600-man infantry cohorts (N = 1.25)

Fort	R	N at given space allowances			Data source
		8 a.q	7 a.q.	6 a.q.	
Caves Inn	11.3	1.1	1.3	**1.5**	Wilson (1972)
Greensforge A	11.4	1.1	1.3	**1.5**	Welfare & Swan (1995)
Prestatyn	12.1	1.2	1.4	1.6	Frere *et al* (1985)
Caerhun	12.5	1.2	1.4	1.6	Webster (1969)
Mean area	11.8 (3.8 acres)				

GROUP FOUR

Forts able to take a 600-man infantry cohort (1.25): a *cohors quingenaria equitata* (N = 1.5) or a *cohors milliaria peditata* (1.666)

Fort	R	N at given space allowances			Data source
		8 a.q	7 a.q.	6 a.q.	
Birrens (Antonine)	12.7	**1.25**	1.4	**1.7**	Johnson (1983)
Vindolanda (Antonine)	12.8	**1.25**	1.4	**1.7**	Birley (1976)
Caerau A 2	13.0	1.3	**1.5**	**1.7**	St Joseph (1969)
Mean area	12.8 (4.1 acres)				

GROUP FIVE

Forts for a *cohors quingenaria equitata* (N = 1.5): a *cohors milliaria peditata* (N = 1.666) or an *ala quingenaria* (N = 2). Two *cohortes quingenariae peditatae* could replace the *ala*.

Fort	R	N at given space allowances			Data source
		8 a.q	7 a.q.	6 a.q.	
Drumlanrigg	14.7	1.4	**1.7**	1.9	Maxwell & Wilson (1987)
Pumpsaint	14.9	**1.5**	**1.7**	1.9	Wilson (1974)
Ribchester	14.9	**1.5**	**1.7**	1.9	Edwards (2000)
Brougham	15.2	**1.5**	**1.7**	**2.0**	Zant (2001)

Fort	R	N at given space allowances			Data source
		8 a.q	7 a.q.	6 a.q.	
Group 5 continued					
Old Carlisle	15.2	**1.5**	**1.7**	**2.0**	Haverfield (1920)
Burrow	15.3	**1.5**	**1.7**	**2.0**	Hildyard (1954)
Manchester 2	15.3	**1.5**	**1.7**	**2.0**	Jones & Grealey (1974)
Ardoch (smaller)	15.5	**1.5**	**1.7**	**2.0**	Breeze (1987)
Greensforge B	15.6	**1.5**	1.8	**2.0**	Welfare & Swan (1995)
Cramond	15.7	**1.5**	1.8	**2.0**	Keppie (1986)
Bothwellhaugh	16.0	1.6	1.8	2.1	Keppie (1986)
Buckton Park	16.2	1.6	1.8	2.1	Welfare & Swan (1995)
Loughor	16.3	1.6	1.8	2.1	Wilson (1971)
Carzield	16.8	**1.7**	1.9	2.2	Keppie (1986)
Vindolanda 1	16.8	**1.7**	1.9	2.2	Bidwell (1999)
Weisbaden	17.0	**1.7**	1.9	2.2	Johnson (1983)
N. Tawton	17.3	**1.7**	1.9	2.2	Welfare & Swan (1995)
Kirkbride	17.5	**1.7**	1.9	2.2	Bellhouse & Richardson (1982)
Mean area	16.0 (5.1 acres)				

GROUP SIX

Forts capable of housing an *alae quingenariae* (N = 2): a *cohors milliaria equitata* (N = 2.666) or smaller units in the appropriate combination.

Fort	R	N at given space allowances			Data source
		8 a.q	7 a.q.	6 a.q.	
Doncaster	19.9	**2.0**	2.2	2.6	Buckland (1978)
Hod Hill	20.2	**2.0**	2.3	**2.7**	Collingwood & Richmond (1969)
Lancaster 1	20.3	**2.0**	2.3	**2.7**	Shotter & White (1995)
Mentieth	20.3	**2.0**	2.3	**2.7**	St Joseph (1974)
Papcastle	20.4	**2.0**	2.3	**2.7**	Birley (1963)
Ardoch (larger)	20.4	**2.0**	2.3	**2.7**	Breeze (1987)
Brompton	20.7	**2.0**	2.3	**2.7**	Welfare & Swan (1995)
Castledykes	20.8	**2.0**	2.3	**2.7**	Keppie (1986)
Median area	20.5 (6.5 acres)				

GROUP SEVEN

Forts capable of taking any unit from a *cohors milliaria equitata* (N = 2.666) to an *ala milliaria* (N = 3 to 4.2) or a combination of smaller units. The median area of this and subsequent groups is not meaningful because the area range is too wide.

Fort	R	N at given space allowances			Data source
		8 a.q	7 a.q.	6 a.q.	
Llwyn y Brain	26.8	**2.6**	3.0	3.5	St Joseph (1969)
Newstead (Flav.)	26.8	**2.6**	3.0	3.5	Collingwood & Richmond (1969)
Blennerhasset	30.2	3.0	3.4	4.0	Evans & Scull (1990)
Lancaster 2	30.7	3.0	3.5	4.0	Shotter & White (1995)
Catterick	30.8	3.0	3.5	4.0	Wilson (1973)
Newstead (Dom.)	31.7	3.1	3.6	**4.2**	Collingwood & Richmond (1969)
Lyne	33.0	3.3	3.7	**4.3**	Collingwood (1922)
London	35.7	3.5	4.0	4.7	Phillips (1977)
Kinvaston 1	40.5	4.0	4.6	5.3	St Joseph (1958)

GROUP EIGHT

Forts to take any combination from an *ala milliaria* to half a legion (N = 4.2 to 6)

Fort	R	N at given space allowances			Data source
		8 a.q	7 a.q.	6 a.q.	
Newstead (Ant.)	42.7	**4.2**	4.8	5.6	Johnson (1983)
Carpow	48.3	4.8	5.4	6.3	St Joseph (1973)

GROUP NINE

Forts to take any combination from half a legion to ten notional cohorts (N = 6 to 12)

Fort	R	N at given space allowances			Data source
		8 a.q	7 a.q.	6 a.q.	
Clifford	54.7	5.4	6.2	7.2	St Joseph (1973)
Alchester	64.0	6.3	7.2	8.4	Sauer (2001)

Fort	R	N at given space allowances			Data source
		8 a.q.	7 a.q.	6 a.q.	
Group Nine cont.d					
Gosbecks	61.4	6.0	6.9	8.1	Wilson (1977)
Longthorpe 1	70.4	7.5	8.5	9.9	Johnson (1983)
Bannaventa	72.0	7.1	8.1	9.5	Wilson (1972)
Longthorpe	75.4	7.5	8.5	9.9	Johnson (1983)

GROUP TEN

Legionary forts (N = 12)

Fort	R	N at given space allowances			Data source
		8 a.q.	7 a.q.	6 a.q.	
Gt. Chesterford	118.8	11.7	13.3	15.5	Rodwell (1972)

Groups 1 to 7 comprise forts that, by and large, housed individual auxiliary units, though sometimes it would have been possible to replace one large unit with two smaller. Table 4.1 shows how each auxiliary unit could fit into more than one fort group. The flexibility inherent in the design is clear.

TABLE 4.1: AUXILIARY UNITS AND THEIR FORTS

(+ Indicates units that could be accommodated at between 6 and 8 a.q. per notional cohort)

Fort Groups	1	2	3	4	5	6	7
Units							
cohors quingenaria peditata	+	+	+				
600-man cohort		+	+	+			
cohors quingenaria equitata			+	+	+		
cohors milliaria peditata				+	+		
ala quingenaria					+	+	
cohors milliaria equitata						+	+
ala milliaria							+

Forts for *alae milliariae*

There is no certainty about the numbers in each of the 24 *turmae* of an *ala milliaria*; 30, 32 or 42. There are therefore several putative models for its fort. Table 4.2 shows 12 options and cites the nearest examples. The values in bold type agree with those observed. It seems that the *Ala Petriana* at Stanwix on Hadrian's Wall comprised 720 (24 x 30) whereas the *Ala II Flavia pia fidelis milliaria* in Germany comprised 1,008 (24 x 42). Niederbieber on the upper German frontier is very similar to Heidenheim but the differences are small enough to be due to scale variations in the published plans.

TABLE 4.2

AREAS WITHIN THE RAMPART (R) AND INTERVALLUM (A) OF PUTATIVE ALA MILLIARIA FORTS

(Areas in a.q.)

Men per turma	30	32	42
Total men	720	768	1008
Notional cohorts	3.0	3.2	4.2
R @ 8 *a.q.*	**30.4** (a)	**32.4** (b)	**42.5** (c)
A @ 8 *a.q.*	24	**25.6** (b)	**33.6** (c)
R @ 6 *a.q.*	22.8	24.3	**32.4** (d)
A @ 6 *a.q.*	18	19.2	25.2

(a) Approximates Stanwix (Dacre 1985): (b) Newstead; Domitianic to Antonine, (Collingwood & Richmond 1969) & Lyne (Collingwood 1922): (c) Heidenheim (Johnson 1983): (d) Niederbieber (Johnson 1983).

TABLE 4.3

FEATURES OF CERTAIN ALA MILLIARIA FORTS

Features	Heidenheim	Niederbieber	Stanwix
Dimensions at inner face of rampart	608 x 865 ft	642 x 872 feet	600 x 700 feet
Area at inner face of rampart (R) in a.q.	36.5	38.9	29.2
Width of *intervallum* (feet)	15 (observed)	33 (observed)	?
Area within the *intervallum* (A) in a.q.	33.5	32.1	-
Notional cohorts at 8 a.q.	4.2 (1,008 men)	4.0 (960 men)	-
Notional cohorts at 6 a.q.	5.6 (1,344 men)	5.35 (1,284 men)	-

Sources: Stanwix, Dacre (1985): Heidenheim, Johnson (1983)

The main features of Heidenheim, Niederbieber and Stanwix are set out in Table 4.3. Heidenheim should have had an *intervallum* of 40 feet surrounding 28.8 *a.q.* but on Johnson's plan it was only about 15 feet which is $1/48^{th}\sqrt{R}$, or $1/46^{th}\sqrt{A}$. But the area within this *intervallum* is 33.5 *a.q.*, enough for 4.2 notional cohorts at 8 *a.q.* This accounts for 1,008 men or 24 *turmae* of 42 and is consistent with an inscription found in the district (Von Domaszcewski 1967). Niederbieber was similar but if the published plan is accurate then it plausibly held a 1008-strong *ala milliaria* at 7.65 *a.q.* (32.1 / 4.2 = 7.65).

The fort at Stanwix is Antonine and measures 600 by 700 feet at its inner rampart; the area (R) is 29.2 *a.q.* or 9.4 acres, significantly smaller than either of the two German forts. A spreadsheet of the various options revealed that 1,008 cavalry would fit only by reducing the *intervallum* to about 32-36 feet and reducing the space allowance to 5.6 *a.q.* This would probably have been unhealthy for horses and awkward for the men and therefore perhaps unlikely. The best option, from a purely numerical point of view, is 720 cavalry within a 30 feet *intervallum* ($1/22 \sqrt{R}$) which fits a space allowance of 8 *a.q.* See Table 4.4.

TABLE 4.4

OPTIONS FOR CAVALRY NUMBERS AT STANWIX

(F = Fractions of $\sqrt{R}$: M = Space allowances: N = Notional cohorts)

F	l (feet)	A (a.q.)	M	N	Cavalry
1/18	36	23.03	8	2.9	696
			6	3.8	912
			5.5	4.2	1,008
1/20	32	23.61	8	2.9	696
			6	3.9	936
			5.6	4.2	1,008
1/22	30	24.1	**8**	**3.0**	**720**
			6	4.0	960
			5.7	4.2	1,008

The several forts at Newstead, Roxburghshire, seem to have been made for a 1008-strong *ala milliaria*, though other units may have occupied the site sometimes. See Table 4.5. This was probably *Ala Augusta Vocontiorum civium Romanorum* which is attested at the site (RIB 2121) or perhaps *Ala Petriana*; both options are possible, given the time span involved.

TABLE 4.5

AREAS OF THE NEWSTEAD FORTS

(R = Area at the rampart: A = Area within the intervallum: N = Notional cohorts)

	R	A	N
Domitianic	31.7	25.1	4.2 at 6.0 a.q.
Antonine 1	32.9	26.0	4.2 at 6.2 a.q.
Antonine 2	32.0	25.6	4.2 at 6.0 a.q.
Means	32.2	25.6	4.2 at 6.0 a.q.

Data from Collingwood & Richmond (1969)

Fortlets

Fortlets may be defined as forts for units of less than one notional cohort. The fort paradigm appears to have been applied but with the *intervallum* rule perhaps sometimes relaxed. Given this uncertainty, and the effect of measurement error with small scale plans, it would be unwise to rely on estimates of the numbers of men in fortlets where the results conflict with other evidence.

TABLE 4.6

NUMBERS OF MEN IN FORTLETS

(R = Area at the ramparts: A = Area within the intervallum: Bold type indicates the probable numbers)

Fortlet	R	A	Space allowance (a.q.) 6		8	
Hardknott	3.73	2.95	**240**		177	
Caerau	1.95	1.50	124	**120**	93	
Castle Shaw	1.79	1.41	113		85	**80**
Highstones	1.28	1.01	81	**80**	**60**	
Lantonside	0.69	0.54	43		32	**30**
Poltross Burn	0.31	0.25	**20**		**15**	

Sources: Hardknott (Collingwood 1928): Caerau (St Joseph 1969): Castle Shaw (Start 1985): Highstones (Hart 1984): Lantonside (Maxwell & Wilson 1987): Poltross Burn (Breeze & Dobson 2000)

Nevertheless, fortlets seem often to have contained one or more centuries of 60 or 80 infantry. Some housed very small detachments (about six men) and space allowances of both 6 and 8 *a.q.* seem to have been applied. Table 4.6 lists a group that represent the sub-divisions of a quingenary infantry cohort, reduced stepwise by halves. The values shown are as derived from the plans, with the probable numbers in bold type. The estimates were obtained by multiplying the derived notional cohort number by 480. Highstones, Derbyshire, demonstrates how the paradigm often allows forts to accommodate the next highest unit by reducing the space allowance from 8 *a.q.* to 6 *a.q.*

Legionary Fortresses

Legionary fortresses are more variable in area than forts. Indeed, it was only by taking data from nine examples that the design constants for a typical legionary fortress could be detected. This suggested that typically each of the 12 notional cohorts of the legion were allowed 12 *a.q.*, giving an area within the *intervallum* (A) of 144 *a.q.* The average *intervallum* width was $1/32^{nd}$ $\sqrt{A}$, i.e. 0.375 *actus*, or 45 feet. This neatly fitted the progression for *intervallum* fractions from $1/8^{th}$ for a camp and $1/16^{th}$ for the fort, and gave the fortress an area of 162 *a.q.* at the rampart. But not one fortress in the series exactly fitted the model, probably because of differing local politico-military circumstances that influenced the storage administrative functions.

Table 4.7 shows the salient features of eight British legionary fortresses arranged in order of area. It is noteworthy that Colchester, presumably the first, is very similar to Inchtuthil which was the last. This implies that area variations were not associated with time but rather with local context. Moreover, the small fortresses like York, Exeter and Usk, are over 20 % smaller than the model, while Gloucester is 16% smaller. York is almost the same as the Great Chesterford fort. There must have been some reason for this state of affairs. Perhaps the smaller fortresses were intended to have relatively short lives, or to contain fewer bureaucrats and fewer stores.

TABLE 4.7: LEGIONARY FORTRESSES IN BRITAIN

(R = Area at the rampart: A = Area within the intervallum: M = Space allowance: Values in brackets are the per-centage variation against the model.)

	R	A	Intervallum (feet)	M (a.q.)
York	120 (-26)	100	58	8.3
Exeter	128 (-21)	113	40	9.5
Usk	128 (-21)	120	20	10.0
Gloucester	137 (-16)	121	36	10.0
Chester	150 (-8)	132	43	11.0
Colchester	170 (+5)	150	46	12.5
Caerleon	170 (+5)	150	46	12.5
Inchtuthil	170 (+5)	150	48	12.5
Means	150 (-7.5)	134	40	11
model	*162*	*144*	*45*	*12*

Sources: York and Chester (Collingwood & Richmond 1969); Exeter (Goodburn 1979); Usk (Frere *et al* 1987); Gloucester (Crummy 1982); Colchester (Crummy 1985); Caerleon and Inchtuthil (Johnson 1983)

Space per man in forts and fortresses

The square footage per man within the *intervallum* (A) in forts and fortresses at various space allowances is shown in Table 4.8. The numbers are those occurring in the composition of the various units; another example of the numerical regularity found in Roman army organisation.

TABLE 4.8: SQUARE FEET PER MAN WITHIN THE INTERVALLUM OF FORTS

S = Space allowance (a.q.)		2	6	8	12
Infantrymen	(S x 14,400) / 480	60	180	240	360
Cavalrymen	(S x 14,400) / 240	120	360	480	720

Manpower and the defence of forts

Since forts had a more generous space allowance than camps, there were relatively fewer men for the defences. Table 4.9 shows the numbers available for each five feet of perimeter and the percentage this represents of a garrison with a space allowance of 8 *a.q.* With the exception of the *ala quingenaria* fort, the rampart could be manned by about half the unit's strength (48% - 64%). This is not a great margin since each man on the rampart had only one replacement. These would have been held as a mobile reserve to rush to points under pressure but if all four sides were assaulted simultaneously, the situation could become perilous and this would explain the elaborate ditch systems seen at many forts. It would also explain why those forts subjected to a determined attack by a numerous enemy could fall. The *ala quingenaria* forts and under-strength units would have been particularly vulnerable.

TABLE 4.9

MEN NEEDED TO MAN THE RAMPARTS OF AUXILIARY FORTS

(One man per five feet of perimeter.)

Unit	Garrison	R (a.q.)	Perimeter (feet)	Men needed	% of garrison
Cohors quingenaria peditata	480	10.1	1,527	305	64
600 man cohort	600	12.7	1,708	342	57
Cohors quingenaria equitata	600	15.2	1,871	374	62
Cohors milliaria peditata	800	16.9	1,971	394	49
Ala quingenaria	480	20.3	2,160	432	90
Cohors milliaria equitata	1,040	27.0	2,494	499	48

Because of the progression that made bigger camps easier to defend (relative reduction in perimeter length), small forts and fortlets would have been very hard pressed to maintain themselves in a seriously hostile environment. Forts with fewer than 200 men would have needed all hands at the rampart. See Table 4.10.

TABLE 4.10

NUMBERS OF MEN NEEDED TO MAN THE RAMPARTS OF FORTLETS

(One man per five feet of perimeter: Space allowance is 6 a.q.)

Total Men	R (a.q.)	Perimeter (feet)	Men needed	% of garrison
400	5.0	1,208	242	60
300	3.8	1,046	209	70
200	2.5	854	171	85
100	1.2	603	121	121
80	1.0	541	108	135
60	0.8	468	94	156

Of course, Roman forts were not redoubts like mediaeval castles, since the Roman habit was not to skulk behind defences but to take the field and swiftly demonstrate who was the master. Nonetheless, situations arose in which the defensive capabilities of forts were put to the test and confirmation of the assessment given above comes from the revolt of Julius Civilis in the Rhineland in AD 70. Early in the disturbances, writes Tacitus (4-14), "...a foolish desperado called Brinno...swooped down on two Roman cohorts in their nearby quarters and simultaneously overran them from the North Sea." These quarters were probably the auxiliary forts at Valkenburg and Katwijk (Wellesley 1964, 213). "The garrison had not expected the attack, nor indeed would it have been strong enough to hold out if it had, so the posts were captured and sacked....The marauders were also on the point of destroying the frontier forts but these were set on fire by the cohort-prefects *because they could not be defended*." (Author's italics)

The two-legion base at Vetera was then attacked by a mixed force of mutineers and tribal war-bands. Tacitus points out that Vetera was never expected to face a siege, though the paradigm ensured that it could be defended by its full garrison of 10,240 infantry. It measured 2,100 x 3,090 feet (17.5 x 225.75 *actus*) (Johnson 1983) so the perimeter was 10,380 feet and under normal circumstances there would be one man per foot of rampart, i.e., each man defending the rampart had four behind him. But, says Tacitus (4-22), "The attacking force was encouraged by the length of the rampart, which was in fact defended by barely 5,000 armed men." This meant there was one man per two feet of perimeter; or for each man spaced at five feet intervals along the rampart, there was only one in reserve. This was the normal situation for an auxiliary fort (Table 4.9) and doubtless knowing this, the commanders did not panic. The fight was desperate, but the depth of the ditches, the stoutness of the walls and resolution of the defenders enabled the legionaries to prevail.

Granaries

Roman forts were furnished with granaries designed to conserve the corn rations of both the men and horses. Grains of corn, being the seeds of plants, are living things that must respire, a process in which they generate energy from the breakdown of carbohydrates. The respiration rate is temperature dependant and the process produces carbon dioxide and water which results in a loss of volume. Stored grain is also subject to attack by insects and moulds as well as rodents. The granary must therefore keep the grain cool, dry and protected from pests. Moreover, because stored grain is bulky and heavy the granary building must have stout walls and a sound roof.

The granary therefore requires proper design and construction to meet these several demands. Usually, though not always, the Roman army granary was stone-built with stout walls to support a heavy, often tiled roof. The walls had external buttresses to help withstand the lateral forces on them due to the weight of grain. The floors were raised above ground level for ventilation and to deter pests. It is certain that many, if not all, had second floors. In ruined forts these structures are usually reduced to their foundations but their areas are a function of the quantities of corn that were stored.

According to information from Polybius, the men received wheat and the horses a wheat-barley mix. The annual quantities are as shown in Table 4.11.

TABLE 4.11

ANNUAL ROMAN ARMY CORN RATIONS ACCORDING TO POLYBIUS

(Col. 2 shows Polybius's monthly figures multiplied by 12: The horse rations are computed by removing the infantryman's ration from that of the respective cavalrymen)

		Attic medimni	Modii (medimni x 6)	Cubic feet (modii / 3)
Infantryman Wheat		8 (0.666 x 12)	48	16
Aux. cavalryman				
	Wheat	16 (1.333 x 12)	96	32
	Barley	60 (5 x 12)	360	120
	Total	76	456	152
Leg. cavalryman				
	Wheat	24 (2 x 12)	144	48
	Barley	84 (7 x 12)	504	168
	Total	108	648	216
Horse rations *				
	Auxiliary	68	408	136
	Legionary	100	600	200

* Note, the legionary cavalry horse has 32 % more corn.

Granaries to hold a year's corn for infantry forts allowed 5 sq. feet of granary floor area per man, such that a quingenary cohort with a ration strength of 500 covered 2,500 sq. feet. It held 50 *modii* per man (25,000 in total). But since the infantryman's annual ration was 48 *modii*, it is likely that two *modii* (4 %) were allowed for loss in storage. In cavalry forts, the floor space allowance was half as much again; 7.5 sq. feet, so a typical quingenary *ala* granary covered 3,600 sq. feet (1/4 *a.q.*). But whereas a one-floor granary could hold an infantry unit's annual supply (24,000 *modii*), a two floored cavalry granary, could hold only 2 x 36,000 *modii*, or 30% of a quingenary *ala*'s theoretical annual requirement of 240,000 *modii* and would need replenishing at least every three to four months. Of course, the horses may not have been fed corn throughout the year but they would if they were to be kept in constant work. They would also have needed hay in winter which would have required barns. The main factor contributing to granary area variation in different forts would appear to be the extent to which the fort served as a depot for other units. An algorithm for estimating the storage potential of granary of known area is given at Appendix Three.

****

CHAPTER FIVE

THE FORTS OF THE FRONTIER WALLS

Introduction

The forts of Hadrian's Wall enjoyed a life of some 300 years. During this time they were periodically refurbished and the outlines of some may have departed somewhat from the original aspect ratio. The occupying units also changed from time to time but there is generally good agreement between the predictions of the paradigm and the units attested from inscriptions. The Antonine Wall forts on the other hand, were only in use for some 30 years, so their outlines are less likely to have deviated from the original plan.

Hadrian's Wall forts

TABLE 5.1

NOTIONAL COHORT SIGNATURES OF HADRIAN'S WALL FORTS

	R	A	\multicolumn{3}{c}{Space allowance}	Predicted unit and whether attested in Breeze and Dobson (2000)	
			8	7	6		
Group 1							
Great Chesters	8.6	6.75	0.85	**1.0**	1.13	c. qu. p.	Yes
Group 2							
Carrawborough	10.5	8.3	1.0	1.2	1.38	c. qu. e.	No
Wallsend	10.7	8.5	1.0	1.2	1.41	c. qu. e.	No
Halton Chesters	10.9	8.6	1.1	1.2	1.44	c. qu. e.	No
means	10.7	8.5	1.0	1.2	1.4		
Group 3							
Rudchester	12.0	9.5	1.2	**1.4**	**1.6**	c. qu. e.	Yes
Carvoran	12.0	9.5	**1.2**	1.4	1.6	c. qu. p.	No
Group 4							
Castlesteads	12.7	10.1	1.26	**1.8**	1.67	c. qu. e.	Yes
Group 5							
Housesteads	14.1	11.0	1.4	**1.6**	1.8	c. m. p	Yes
Chesters	15.5	12.2	1.5	1.8	**2.0**	Ala. qu.	Yes
Birdoswald	15.6	12.3	**1.5**	1.75	2.0	c. p. m.	Yes
Benwell	16.9	13.3	1.67	**1.9**	**2.2**	Ala. qu.	Yes
Bewcastle	17.0	13.4	**1.68**	1.9	2.2	c. p. m.	Yes
Bowness	17.0	13.4	1.68	1.9	2.4	c. p.m.?	?
means	16.0	12.6	1.5	1.8	2.1		

Table 5.1 lists the forts according to the classification suggested in Chapter Four. The abbreviations are; Ala = *ala;* c = *cohors;* p = *peditata;* e = *equitata;* qu = *quingenaria;* m = *milliaria.* Stanwix is omitted because it was discussed with the *ala milliaria* forts. The data are as derived from published plans and most of the units' signatures are instantly recognisable.[1] Whether or not these agree with the units attested is shown in the last column. Newcastle, Drumburgh and Burgh by Sands, apparently made for less than one notional cohort, are classed as fortlets and discussed separately.

Group One: Great Chesters: This fort is ideal for a *cohors quingenaria peditata.*

Group Two: Carrawborough, Wallsend and Halton Chesters could take one notional cohort at 8 *a.q.* so the presence of *cohortes quingenariae equitatae* suggests that cavalry were included after the fort perimeter had been fixed. This gave them a space allowance of 5.666 *a.q.*

Group Three: Carvoran and Rudchester appear to have been intended for *cohortes quingenariae peditatae*, including 600-man infantry cohorts (N = 1.25), and *cohortes quingenariae equitatae* (N = 1.5). *Cohors I Hamiorum Sagittarium* was stationed at Carvoran and if it comprised one notional cohort then its space allowance was 9.5 *a.q.* There are not other auxiliary forts with such a generous provision and the strong inference is that the Hamian archers were 600-strong (N = 1.25).

Group Four: Castlesteads could take any unit from an infantry cohort of 600 (N = 1.25) to a milliary infantry cohort (N = 1.666). The unit thought to have been present under Hadrian, *cohors IV Gallorum equitata,* if quingenary, would have fitted at 6.66 *a.q.* In the 3rd century, *cohors II Tungorum equitata* is attested and is thought to have been milliary (Breeze & Dobson 2000, 268). Such a unit (N = 2.666) would not have fitted Castlestead's known outline without a dire squeeze. But this unit was at half strength in Bavaria in the Hadrianic and Antonine periods so the other half may have been at Castlesteads, though this seems an odd arrangement.

Group Five: Housesteads, Chesters, Birdoswald, Benwell, Bewcastle and Bowness: For Bowness, Breeze and Dobson (2000) suggested a milliary unit, possibly *equitata*. The area is right for a milliary cohort *peditata* at 8 *a.q.* but if the *equitate* unit were present, its space allowance was 5.0 *a.q.*, which seems somewhat restricting. A possible explanation is that part of the unit was at nearby Burgh by Sands; see below. The *cohors milliaria peditata* attested at Birdoswald may have been intended for that fort, at 7.4 *a.q.* (12.3 / 1.666) but it could take a *cohors quingenaria equitata* at 8 *a.q.* or an *ala quingenaria* at 6 *a.q.* It is not easy to be certain which unit was intended for Housesteads since the standard space allowances do not give a clear signature. The *cohors peditata milliaria* attested had a space allowance of 6.6 *a.q.* (11 / 1.666).

Hadrian's Wall fortlets

Table 5.2 lists the salient features of three fortlets. The outline of the Newcastle fort is not known for certain. Frere *et al* (1986) suggested a plan consistent with option (a) but the only certain dimension on their plan is the *via principalis* of 1.75 *actus*. When the fort is re-modelled on the spreadsheet for several aspect ratios using this dimension as the width, the most plausible option is (b); a 4 by 5 aspect ratio for 0.5 notional cohorts (240 infantry) at 6 *a.q.* The differences between the two options are not great

Like Newcastle, Burgh by Sands and Drumburgh fortlets are atypical and the latter's history is uncertain. Their areas preclude them from containing any complete unit. Given the space allowances applying elsewhere on the Wall, they could have held between 240 and 320 infantry, or between 120 and 160 cavalry; or combinations of both. It is possible that a *cohors quingenaria peditata* was divided between the two. An alternative explanation, already mentioned, is that detachments from the putative *cohors milliaria equitata* at nearby Bowness were housed at Burgh by Sands and Drumburgh. The total area within the *intervallum* of all three forts is 21.4 *a.q.* (13.4 + 4 + 4). This area would take the full unit at 8 *a.q.* (21.4 / 2.666 = 8.0). This is very persuasive. The notional cohort division between the forts would be: Bowness, 1.666, (800 infantry) Burgh by Sands 0.5 (120 cavalry), Drumburgh, 0.5 (120 cavalry). Of course, this hypothesis assumes that all three forts were operational at the same time, which they may not have been.

TABLE 5.2: HADRIAN'S WALL FORTLETS

(R=Area within the rampart: A = Area within the intervallum)

Fortlet	R	A	Space allowance			Attested Unit and signature
			8	7	6	
Newcastle (a)	5.9	4.6	0.6	0.7	0.8	?
Newcastle (b)	3.8	3.0	0.4	0.4	0.5	?
Burgh - Sands	5.1	4.0	0.5	0.6	0.666	?
Drumburgh	5.0	4.0	0.5	0.6	0.666	?

Space allowances on Hadrian's Wall

Table 5.3 shows that the mean space allowance per notional cohort on Hadrian's Wall was 6.6 *a.q.* (standard deviation = 0.9). The three fortlets are omitted because of uncertainty about their garrisons.

TABLE 5.3

SPACE ALLOWANCES IN THE FORTS OF HADRIAN'S WALL

(A = Area within the intervallum)

Fort	A (a.q.)	Signature of unit attested	Space allowance (a.q.)
Stanwix	24.1	3.0	8.0
Bewcastle	13.4	1.666	8.0
Benwell	13.3	2.0	6.6
Bowness	13.4	2.666 ?	5.0
Chesters	12.2	2.0	6.1
Birdoswald	12.3	1.666	7.4
Housesteads	11.0	1.666	6.6
Castlesteads	10.1	1.5	6.7
Rudchester	9.5	1.5	6.33
Carvoran	9.5	1.25	7.6
Wallsend	8.5	1.5	5.66
Halton Chesters	8.6	1.5	5.7
Carrawborough	8.3	1.5	5.5
Great Chesters	6.75	1.0	6.75
Mean			6.6
Standard Dev'n			0.9

The Antonine Wall forts

The Antonine Wall was about half the length of Hadrian's Wall and had six "primary" forts and 16 fortlets, though the data concerning their total acreage is incomplete. Table 5.4 lists eight forts that could have taken at least one notional cohort. The values in bold type are those which agree with the units attested from inscriptions. The mean space allowance was 7.0 *a.q.* (74.4 / 10.67) which is 0.4 *a.q.* more than the mean for Hadrian's Wall, but within its standard deviation.

TABLE 5.4

NOTIONAL COHORTS IN THE ANTONINE WALL FORTS

(R = Area within the rampart in a.q.: A = Area within the intervallum in a.q.: Best option)

	R	A	Signatures			BO	Suggested unit	Whether attested
			8	7	6			
1. O Kilpatrick	12.7	10.0	1.25	1.4	**1.666**	1.666	c. m. p.	yes
2. Bearsden	7.3	5.8	0.7	0.8	**1.0**	1	c. qu. p.	?
3. Balmuidy	9.9	7.8	**1.0**	1.1	1.3	1	c. qu. p.	yes
4. Cadder	8.1	6.4	0.8	0.9	**1.1**	1	c. qu. p.	yes
5. Bar Hill	10.1	8.0	**1.0**	1.1	1.33	1	c. qu. p.	yes
6. Castlecary	10.8	8.5	**1.1**	1.2	1.4	1	c. qu. p.	various inf. units
7. Mumrills	20.4	16.1	**2.0**	2.3	2.7	2	Ala qu.	yes
8. Carriden	12.5	11.8	1.5	1.7	**2.0**	2	Ala qu.	?
Totals		74.4				10.666		

Sources: (1, 4, 6) MacDonald (1934): (2,8) Breeze & Dobson (2000): (3, 7) Johnson (1983): (5) Keppie (1986):

****

---

[1] The sources for the data of the Hadrian's Wall forts are as follows: Bowness, Frere *et al* (1989): Burgh by Sands, Drumburgh, Collingwood Bruce (1966): Castlesteads, Carvoran, Bewcastle, Birdoswald, Halton Chesters, Housesteads, Chesters, Rudchester, Benwell, Wallsend, Bidwell (1999): Great Chesters, Breeze and Dobson (2000)

CHAPTER SIX

THE DEPLOYMENT OF ROMAN ARMIES IN THE FIELD

Numbers and distribution of camps in England

Considering the period of 800 or so years during which the Roman army made camps, it is surprising that more sites are not known. This is probably due to ramparts weathering away and ditches silting up, even when they have not been deliberately destroyed by farming. Nevertheless, although hundreds must await discovery we now have sufficient examples to draw some tentative conclusions about how they were used and about their possible historic contexts.

TABLE 6.1

DISTRIBUTION OF ROMAN CAMPS IN ENGLAND

(After Welfare & Swan 1995)

County	No of camps
Cumbria	27
Devon	2
Co Durham	7
Lincolnshire	3
Norfolk	1
Northumberland	54
North Yorkshire	7
Nottinghamshire	5
Shropshire	16
Somerset	1
Staffordshire	13
Total	136

Welfare & Swan (1995) have listed 136 camps at 95 sites in England. See Table 6.1. The main clusters are near Wroxeter; along the Carlisle - York road in Cumbria and along Hadrian's Wall and Dere Street in Northumberland. There is a wide scatter in Yorkshire and a smaller one in Nottinghamshire, but only one example south and east of the Fosse Way (Horstead, Norfolk). This is a very uneven distribution and the absence of camps in southern England is very noticeable. Most of the soils in the south readily produce crop marks and much of the area has been surveyed from the air. Some consider this good evidence for the Romans having not made camps in southern England, the Romans having overrun the southern tribes without much resistance. This possibility is supported by a statement of Bede, who claimed that Claudius, "...within a few days, without battle or bloodshed ... received the surrender of the greater part of the island."

This interpretation conflicts with the notion of Roman forces making camps in all circumstances, even when stopping in the field for a single night. Nor does it square with the idea of hard fought actions, particularly in Kent, Hertfordshire and Essex. The absence of camps in southern England may well be due to chance, with many awaiting discovery, but this seems unlikely. It is more likely, therefore, that the conquest was relatively easy with the army often sparing itself the labour of digging defensive ditches. A sentence of Josephus (III, 71) supports this possibility. At the conclusion of his account of the camp, where he mentions the rampart, he writes, "*If necessary*, (author's italics) a ditch is dug all round, six feet deep and the same width." This implies that the ditch was not obligatory and that the army could sometimes camp behind palisades that have left no trace. Such a practice could have given rise to the term "picket", literally a pointed stake inserted into the ground, but one that has become synonymous with a line of sentries. There is also some other evidence that camps were not fortified when action was not expected, though it concerns the deplorable state that Aulus Albinus allowed his army to fall into in 108-109 BC in the Jugurthine War. "The camps were not fortified," wrote Sallust, "nor were watches posted in accordance with military routine; and men absented themselves from duty whenever they pleased." (Handford 1963).

The camps in the rest of Britain pose some interesting questions. Many must have been made on active service but some must have been practice works. However, it will not be possible to distinguish them without such significant clues as those found at Burnswark, Dumfriesshire, which suggested the site was used for siege exercises (Keppie 1986, 79). Bearing in mind these reservations, the following sections suggest how questions of historical context might be approached.

Spreadsheets to investigate the provenance of Roman camps

The area and dimensions of the camp for a given number of notional cohorts can be found with the *synthesis* spreadsheet. This can be used iteratively, i.e., to test different notional cohort numbers against the dimensions of a known camp. It uses the equations set out at the end of Chapter Three and a specimen for a camp of three notional cohorts is shown at Table 6.2. To calculate the dimensions of the axes of oblong camps, the formulae given in Chapter Three must be applied.

TABLE 6.2

SYNTHESIS SPREADSHEET OF A CAMP

(The single in-put is in bold type: Dimensions are in actus: Areas are in a.q. unless specified)

Features	Formulae and data	Print out
Total notional cohorts (N)	**N = 3**	3.0
Strigae (S)	N x 1.5	4.5
Multiplier (m)	1.333	-
Area within *intervallum* (A)	S m, or N x 2	6.0
Length of inner margin of *intervallum*	$\sqrt{A}$	2.45
Width *of intervallum* (I)	$(\sqrt{A})/8$	0.30
Width of *intervallum* (I) in feet	$[(\sqrt{A})/8] \times 120$	37
Length at inner margin of rampart (L)	$(\sqrt{A}) + 2I$	3.05
Area at inner margin of rampart (R)	L x L	9.30
Area at the rampart in acres	R x 0.3215	3.0

It is easier to find the number of notional cohorts for a given camp by starting with its dimensions and working backwards. This requires the *analysis* model whereby the spreadsheet is written to convert the dimensions of the base rectangle measured in millimetres from the scale plan, into *actus* and Roman feet and then to estimate the notional cohort number. Aspect ratio makes no difference to the estimate. The equations are:

1. Length x width, in *actus*, at the inner face of the rampart = R
2. *Intervallum* (I) = ($\sqrt{R}$) / 10
3. Area within *intervallum* (A) = $(\sqrt{R} - 2I)^2$
4. Area of *strigae* (S) = A / 1.333
5. Notional cohorts (N) = A/2, or S/1.5

For the best results, a good plan is required and the bigger the scale, the better. The first step is to define the base rectangle. With parallelograms or asymmetrical outlines this can be done with a pencil, ruler and set square, but some trial and error may be needed. Often one corner of the camp is a right angle and this is a good place to start. Where there are parallel sides, the perpendicular distance between them should be measured. The *decumanus* may be taken as the straight distance between the central gates in the short sides. Some examples were shown in Figure 3.1. Once the rectangle is defined, the lengths of *cardo* and *decumanus* can be measured in millimetres and the values inserted into the spreadsheet.

For small camps (less than four notional cohorts) the *analysis* spreadsheet may reveal the signatures of individual units but with bigger camps the permutations become too great, and as the area increases, the effect of scale error is magnified. Nevertheless, notional cohort numbers estimated from base rectangles are better guides to occupying forces than are acreages over the ramparts.

TABLE 6.3

A SPECIMEN SPREADSHEET OF QUATT CAMP

(Data from Welfare & Swan 1995: In puts in bold type: Print-outs in column 2: Formulae in column 3.)

Plan scale	**40** mm (a)	**100** metres (b)
		1mm = (b/a) x 0.028 = 0.140 = (q)
Mean dimensions at inner face of rampart		
Cardo	**18 mm**	18 x q = C
Decumanus	**27 mm**	27 x q = D
Area at inner rampart (R)	9.65	C x D = R
Intervallum	0.31 (37 feet)	($\sqrt{R}$)/100 = I (x 120 = feet)
Area within *intervallum* (A)	6.1	$(\sqrt{R} - 2I)^2 = A$
Strigae (S)	4.6	A x 0.75 = S
Notional cohorts (N)	3.0	S / 1.5 = N

Table 6.3 shows a spreadsheet of the camp at Quatt, Shropshire. It has a 2:3 aspect ratio and a regular outline. There are four possible options for the three notional cohorts it sheltered;

1. Three *cohortes peditatae quingenariae*, legionary or auxiliary; (3 x 1)
2. Two *cohortes quingenariae equitatae*; (2 x 1.5)
3. One *cohors peditatae quingenaria* and an *ala quingenaria*; (1 + 2)
4. One *Ala milliaria* with 24 *turmae* of 30 men, totalling 720; (3)

Appendix Two lists 113 camps whose notional cohort numbers have been estimated from published plans.

Camps for less than one notional cohort

Table 6.4 lists seven camps that appear to be the work of under-strength quingenary infantry cohorts, though cavalry may have been present in some, replacing the infantry at the rate of one *turma* to 60 infantry. These findings suggest that the paradigm was applied even with small numbers which is, of course, to be expected since manpower restraints were most acute in small camps.

TABLE 6.4: CAMPS FOR LESS THAN ONE NOTIONAL COHORT

(After Richardson 2002)

Camp	Area a.q.	Notional cohorts (N) calculated	Notional cohorts (N) probable	Infantrymen (N prob. x 480)	Centuries
Grindon School	1.0	0.32	0.333	160	2 x 80
Coesike East	1.7	0.50	0.50	240	4 x 60 or 3 x 80
Grindon Hill	1.1	0.50	0.50	240	4 x 60 or 3 x 80
Coesike West 1	2.0	0.64	0.64	307	5 x 60
Masada A	1.45	0.73	0.75	360	6 x 60
Bowes Moor	2.63	0.75	0.75	360	6 x 60
Swine Hill 2	2.57	0.82	0.82	394	5 x 80

Camps for single units

Table 6.5 lists some camps that appear to be the work of single auxiliary units.

TABLE 6.5: CAMPS FOR SINGLE AUXILIARY UNITS

(N = Notional cohort number)

Unit	N	Examples
Cohors peditata quingenaria	1.0	Brown Dykes and Sunny Rigg
Cohors peditata 600 men	1.25	Nowtler Hill 1
Cohors equitata quingenaria	1.5	Walwick Fell, Willowford, Golden Fleece, Sunny Rigg 2
Cohors peditata milliaria	1.666	Troutbeck 3, Haltwhistle Burn 2, Moss Side 1
Cohors equitata milliaria	2.666	Hoole, Grange Moat
Ala quingenaria (16 x 32 men)	2.13	Langwathby
Ala milliaria (24 x 30 men)	3.0	Quatt, Glenwhelt Leazes
Ala milliaria (24 x 42 men)	4.2	Lees Hall, Calverton 2, Sills Burn N & S

Sources: Dimensions of Hoole and Grange Moat from Philpott (1998) after allowing for rampart and berm: all other camps from Richardson (2002)

The one-legion army group

Roman legions normally took to the field accompanied by auxiliary units. The ancient literature tells us nothing about the theoretically ideal combination; though Vegetius suggests about 5,000 auxiliaries were attached to a legion. A statistical study (Richardson 2001) of the relative numbers of camps in different area categories has, however, given an insight into the matter and is summarised in this section.

Welfare and Swan (1995) published a bar-chart showing that in England, the smaller the camp, the more frequently it occurred. Indeed, the relationship was consistent with an army being continually halved to produce twice the number of sub-formations. This was analogous to the decay curve of a drug in the blood stream after a single dose and meant that a graph plot of the number of camps in each area category against the *logarithm* of the areas would give a straight line. Furthermore, the point at which the line cut the area axis of the graph (intercept) would be analogous to the drug dose before its degradation in the body; that is, the logarithm of the area of the camp that was the "parent" of all the others.

The "parent" camp was found to be 100 *a.q.* or 32 acres, enough for 32 notional cohorts, and was remarkable for its numerical simplicity. The men occupied 48 *a.q.* of *strigae* (32 x 1.5) within an area of 64 *a.q* (8 x 8 *actus*) defined by an *intervallum* exactly one *actus* wide, which gave dimensions of 10 x 10 *actus* at the inner face of the rampart. In England, there are only three examples of such a camp; East Learmouth (Northumberland), Greensforge (Staffordshire) and Norton 1 (Shropshire).

This 32-notional cohort army almost certainly consisted of a legion (12 notional cohorts) and 20 notional cohorts of auxiliaries. Typically, though not invariably, about half were cavalry; that is, half in notional cohort terms, not numbers of men. Ten notional cohorts of infantry number 4,800, whereas ten notional cohorts of cavalry number 2,400. A study of the armies mentioned in various passages of Tacitus and Josephus suggested this was probably the standard formation, though in practice there were often shortfalls, particularly of cavalry (Richardson 2001). The references to these forces largely concerned situations in civil war and rebellion where armies were thrown together in moments of crisis, so perhaps in less desperate times the desired auxiliary contingents did accompany the legions.

The two-legion army group

The largest camp in England, Brampton Bryan, Herefordshire, covers 64 acres and would have held two such legionary army formations. These were possibly under the command of the governor, Julius Frontinus on his way to subdue the Silures of South Wales in the 70s AD. A situation that was not an obvious emergency was Agricola's Mons Graupius campaign. Tacitus reported that he had 8,000 auxiliary infantry and 5,000 cavalry, which would have amounted to 37.5 notional cohorts; thus,

$$8000 / 480 = 16.666$$
$$5000 / 240 = 20.8$$
$$\text{Total} \quad 37.5$$

If Agricola had been accompanied by two legions (24 notional cohorts), his camps would have held 61.5 notional cohorts and covered 61.5 x 0.981 = 60.33 acres. This strongly suggests he was responsible for the series of "63-acre" camps in Scotland, because when the calculations are made with a presumption that Agricola had 64 (2 x 32) notional cohorts, the camps would be 63 acres (64 x 0.981). The small notional cohort discrepancy could be explained by Tacitus having simply stated approximate figures; 600 fewer infantry and 300 fewer cavalry; quite understandable in a eulogy written some years after the event.

This two-legion army was the direct descendent of the consular army of the republic and it is instructive to compare the two. Table 6.6 lists the numbers in both. Overall, there was a considerable (8%) saving on manpower in the imperial army, but it had more legionary infantry while the non-citizen infantry was drastically cut. At the same time, the legionary cavalry were so reduced as to suggest it was confined to legionary duties, perhaps as the legate's bodyguard, while the auxiliary cavalry was increased by a third. In the light of the changes in the paradigm constants which released more men from construction and defensive roles, this restructuring points to the more aggressive role being taken up by the auxiliary cavalry.

TABLE 6.6

THE CONSULAR ARMY OF THE REPUBLIC AND THE IMPERIAL TWO-LEGION ARMY

Component	Republic	Empire	Change
Legionary infantry	8,400	10,240	1,840 more (+ 22 %)
Non citizen infantry	8,400	4,800	3,600 less (- 43 %)
Legionary cavalry	600	240	360 less (- 60 %)
Non citizen cavalry	1,800	2,400	600 more (+ 33.33 %)
Totals	19,200	17,680	1,520 less (- 8 %)

It also a curious fact that if we take the 150 *a.q.* tented area of the Polybian camp and fill it at the space allowances of the imperial army, we find that it would take exactly 100 notional imperial cohorts; thus, $150 / 1.5 = 100$.

Sub-divisions of a legionary army

Most camps in England sheltered fewer than 32 notional cohorts, suggesting that most of the action in Britain south of the Cheviots was against small tribal groups, or involved police duties. When the 32-notional cohort legionary army began to split, presumably to hold down a semi-pacified territory, it gave two sub-groups of 16 notional cohorts and then four of eight; then eight of four notional cohorts and finally 16 of two. Some examples (from Appendix 2) are:

16	Milestone House, Seatsides 1, St Harmon
8	Gleadthorpe, Dun, Bagraw South
4	Lees Hall
2	Upton 6

These sub-divisions were sometimes re-combined to give forces of 12, 20 and 24 notional cohorts. For example;

12 (8 + 4)	Wath, Kirkby Thore 1
20 (16 + 4)	Rey Cross, Chew Green 1, Malham
24 (16 + 8)	Inchtuthil camp, Mentieth, Walford

The force that entered Cumberland from Yorkshire, via the Stainmore gap, probably making the camps at Rey Cross, Crackenthorpe and Plumpton Head, comprised 20 notional cohorts; probably a legion and eight notional cohorts of auxiliaries. At Plumpton Head, this force may have split in two; one half making the 10-acre Troutbeck 1 camp, at the head of the vale of Keswick, and the other half heading for the lower Eden valley to make the 10-acre camp, Moss Side 2, near Brampton. The two halves may then have re-grouped and returned east of the Pennines via the 20-acre camp at Fell End on the Stanegate. The deployment of multiples of ten notional cohorts may have been customary in the north throughout the Flavian period because the later, larger camp Troutbeck 2, Cumbria, and Bellshiel and both Featherwood camps (E & W) in Northumberland, were for 40 notional cohorts. For a fuller discussion, see Richardson (2003b).

Camps for an augmented legionary army

A one-legion army group (32 notional cohorts) could be combined with sub-groups of other legionary army groups, thus:

36	(32 + 4)	Caerau (probably)
38	(32 + 6)	Stracathro, Swindon, Burlington
40	(32 + 8)	Featherwood E. & W, Bellshiel
44	(32 + 12)	Uffington 1

The British auxiliary garrison under Hadrian

Breeze and Dobson (2000, 163) reported that the auxiliary garrison of Britain under Hadrian numbered 59 units, stationed on the frontier or behind it in reserve. Fifty nine seems an odd number, bearing in mind the Roman army's apparent liking for numerical neatness, and especially since the likely figure of 60 would give 20 units to each legion – 20 units, note, not 20 notional cohorts. The apparently missing unit is probably a *cohors milliaria peditata*, because if one were included in the list, the auxiliary garrison would be composed as shown in Table 6.7.

TABLE 6.7

THE PUTATIVE BRITISH AUXILIARY GARRISON UNDER HADRIAN

(N = Notional cohorts)

Type of unit	Number	N (infantry)	N (cavalry)	(N) Totals
Cohortes peditatae quingenariae	12	12	-	12
Cohortes peditatae milliariae	3	5	-	5
Cohortes equitatae quingenariae	24	24	12	36
Cohortes equitatae milliariae	5	8.333	5	13.333
Alae quingenariae	15	-	30	30
Alae milliariae	1	-	3	3
Totals	60	49.33	50	99.33

This garrison was divided between the frontier and a reserve stationed at various places within the province. Those of Hadrian's Wall and the Cumberland coastal forts comprised 31.8 (32) notional cohorts, (19.33 infantry and 12.5 cavalry), the equivalent of a legionary army group. Indeed, if the Carvoran garrison was a 600-strong *cohors quingenaria peditata* as the signature of 1.2 suggests (Table 5.1), the total would be exactly 32 notional cohorts. This suggests that the frontier line might have been managed as a distinct entity. See Table 6.8.

TABLE 6.8

THE GARRISON OF THE BRITISH HADRIANIC FRONTIER

(After Breeze & Dobson 2000 and Richardson 2001)

Fort	Unit	Notional cohorts			
		Infantry	Cavalry	Totals	
Infantry only					
Newcastle	c.q.p.	1	-	1	
Housesteads	"	1.666	-	1.666	
Great Chesters	"	1	-	1	
Carvoran	"	1	-	1	
Birdoswald	"	1.666	-	1.666	
Bewcastle	"	1.666	-	1.666	
Beckfoot	"	1	-	1	
Sub total		(9)	-		9
Cavalry only					
Chesters	a.q.	-	2		
Benwell	"	-	2		
Stanwix	a.m	-	3		
Sub total			(7)		7
Mixed units					
Wallsend	c.q.e.	1	0.5	1.5	
Rudchester	"	1	0.5	1.5	
Halton Chesters	"	1	0.5	1.5	
Carrawborough	"	1	0.5	1.5	
Castlesteads	"	1	0.5	1.5	
Burgh by Sands	"	1	0.5	1.5	
Bowness	c.m.e.	1.666	1	2.666	
Maryport	"	1.666	1	2.666	
Moresby	c.q.e.	1	0.5	1.5	
Sub total		(10.33)	(5.5)		15.83
Grand Total					31.8

The whole British auxiliary garrison was therefore partitioned between the frontier and reserve as shown in Table 6.9.

TABLE 6.9

DISTRIBUTION OF THE BRITISH HADRIANIC AUXILIARY GARRISON IN NOTIONAL COHORTS

(Numbers of men in brackets)

Location	Infantry	Cavalry	Totals
Frontier	20 (9,600)	12 (2,880)	32 (12,480)
Reserve	30 (14,400)	38 (9,120)	68 (23,520)
Totals	50 (24,000)	50 (12,000)	100 (36,000)

Because the grand total is 100 notional cohorts, the actual values are also percentages. It is immediately clear that virtually a third were deployed on the frontier where the proportion of infantry (in notional cohort terms) was greater than in the reserve: 62 % (20/32), compared with 44 % (30/68). One hundred notional cohorts, equally split into infantry and cavalry, is unlikely to be an accidental arrangement and looks like another example of numerical harmony intruding into, what to us, would be a purely pragmatic problem. When gathered together this garrison would need a camp of 100 acres, and when combined with the three British legions (36 notional cohorts), it would need one of 133 acres; i.e., 136 x 0.981. Therefore, any significantly larger camp than this in Britain probably included reinforcements from the Continent.

Large camps in Scotland

Scotland has several large camps which have invited speculation on their historic contexts, most notably by St Joseph (1969, 1973, 1977), who has outlined some putative campaigns based on a comparison of their acreages, and by Hanson (1977-78). But comparing areas over the ramparts is less accurate than comparing the areas of base rectangles, or the derived notional cohort values. For example, St Joseph estimated Rae Dykes at 93 acres, but even from the small-scale plan of Collingwood and Richmond (1969) it can be seen to be a 5:6 rectangle whose long axis may be defined from the mean distance between opposite gates in the short sides. See Figure 3.1. The long axis is 2,280 feet (19 *actus*) at the inner face of the rampart and the short axis is 1,900 feet, (15.833 *actus*), so the outer rectangle (R) is 300 *a.q.*, or 96 acres. The *intervallum* would be 208 feet enclosing 192 *a.q.* within which were 192 x ¾ = 144 *a.q* of *strigae* for the 96 (3 x 32) notional cohorts of a three-legion army group.

Nevertheless, it is possible to detect a pattern of multiples of eight notional cohorts in much of St Joseph's data. See Table 6.10.

TABLE 6.10

APPROXIMATE ACREAGES OF SOME CAMPS IN SCOTLAND

(After St Joseph 1969, 1973, 1977: Areas in brackets are differences between the groups.)

	Approximate acreage	Examples
	24	Dornoch, Mentieth, Dalginross
(8)		
	32	Dunblane, Ardoch
(8)		
	40	Stracathro, Castledykes
(24)		
	64	19 camps listed by St Joseph (1973, 230)
(24)		
	96	Rae Dykes
(16)		
	112	Ythan wells, Dunning
(16)		
	128	Grassy Walls, Cardean
(16)		
	144	Durno
(16)		
	160	Newstead

The largest camp at Ardoch (7) (St Joseph 1977) has a base rectangle at the ramparts of 394 *a.q.* (122 acres) for 124 notional cohorts, or three 32-notional cohort groups plus another 28 notional cohorts. This is virtually four legionary armies. Such a force almost equalled the whole garrison of Britain and the likely contexts for such armies are the Severan campaigns.

Table 6.11 lists camps comprising multiples of 32 notional cohorts, including two that might have held the whole British garrison (Innerpeffray and Cardean).

TABLE 6.11

PUTATIVE LEGIONARY ARMIES IN SCOTLAND

Notional cohorts	Possible examples (acres)
32 (1 x 32)	Dunblane (34) Bonnytown (35) Ythan Wells (35)
64 (2 x 32)	St Joseph's "63 acre" series
96 (3 x 32)	Rae Dykes (96)
128 (4 x 32)	? Balmakewan (123)
136 (4 x 12 + 8)	Innerpeffray (136) Cardean (136)
160 (5 x 32)	? St Joseph's "165 acre" series

The 120-acre camps in Scotland

St Joseph (1973) compiled a group of twelve "120-acre" camps, listed in Table 6.12. They are a far from homogenous group and average 120 acres only because they include examples covering a 40-acre range; from 93 (Rae Dykes) to 136 (Innerpeffray and Cardean). There is not a 120-acre camp in the whole set and the variation is enough to account for 40 notional cohorts. This stretches the concept of an average beyond the limit of meaning. These camps seem to comprise six sub-sets. The *median* (value in the middle of the range) is 122 acres. The difference between this and each camp's area (column 4) reveals the sub-sets more clearly and for the most part they correspond to halves and quarters of a legionary army group. The mean notional cohort number of Group 5 is 110, virtually that of the Hyginian camp.

TABLE 6.12

ST JOSEPH'S "120-ACRE" CAMPS IN SCOTLAND

(N = Notional cohorts = Acres / 0.981: D = Difference from the median in acres)

Camp	Acres	N	D	N (probable)
Group 1				
Innerpeffray	136	138.6	17	138
Cardean	136	138.6	17	138
Group 2				
Kair House	130	132.5	8	132
Oathlaw	130	132.5	8	132
Grassy Walls	129	131.5	7	132
Group 3				
Balmakewan	123	125.3	1	124
Ardoch 7	122	124.3	0	124
Group 5				
Ythan Wells	111	113.1	-11	112
Kintore	110	112.1	-12	110
Muiryfold	109	111.1	-13	110
Normandykes	106	108.0	-16	108
Group 6				
Rae Dykes	93	95	-29	96
Mean	120			
Median	122			
Range	43			

Much work remains to be done with regard to the possible historical contexts of camps and it is to be hoped that more accurate plans will become available. An inventory of camps in Scotland similar to that produced for England by the Royal Commission of Historic Monuments would be an invaluable aid in the task of distinguishing Flavian, Antonine and Severan camps.

****

CHAPTER SEVEN

GENERAL DISCUSSION

The evidence set out in this book shows that the Romans approached the organisation of their armies and the problems of camp and fort design with a sound understanding of *ergonomics*; that is with a grasp of the quantifiable aspects of a soldier's effort in terms of both manual labour and combat. Whether they had a word for this apparently modern notion is an interesting question but there can be no doubt they understood the concept. They also understood a number of others for which we must use modern terminology; *man-hours*, *work rate* and *optimum deployment of resources* and they used mathematics to manipulate them into a workable paradigm. Besides simple addition, multiplication, squares and square roots, they also applied what we would now call *transformations* to avoid calculating with very large numbers; working *actus* rather than feet and notional cohorts rather than numbers of men. But more than that, they worked to mathematical ideals of harmony discovered by Greek intellectuals.

This methodology seems to have formed the core of their military science from the early days of the republic down to the last years of the western empire and must have been maintained by a body of experts who knew how to write what we should call *standard operating procedures*. These men must have formed some sort of military bureaucracy who presumably had offices and kept archives. They would have trained those aspiring to the rank of *praefectus castrorum*, many of whom became *agrimensores* after their military service, supervising the allocation of agricultural land. Though not steeped in the sciences, these men were nevertheless literate and familiar with the basics of arithmetic and geometry (Dilke 1971).

It seems unlikely that the patricians who took senior military appointments during their careers in the public service studied all the details of military science. But the best of them had a sound grasp of what it could achieve. The most notable must be Julius Caesar whose commentaries reveal that he thought in terms of entrenchments and camps as much as of flanking movements, force concentration and the assault. As an aristocrat, he doubtless had a lofty detachment from the planners and engineers who were the organising brains of his army. For example, he gave details of the bridge *he* threw over the Rhine, knowing how this would impress his countrymen, as it had the barbarians, but said nothing of the men whose skills actually brought it about. Nor did he refer to the staff work that must have preceded the great sieges of Gergovia and Alesia, or the invasions of Britain. Indeed, in the winter before his second invasion he cleared off to Italy and left the job to his underlings. The military engineer, like the common soldier, appears to have been taken very much for granted. The disdain shown by ancient aristocrats towards these intellectual artisans was probably akin to that of their modern counterparts who, while despising wealthy industrialists, have not shrunk from marrying their daughters. They affected scorn to conceal their gratitude.

****

APPENDIX ONE

This translation was made by I. A. Richmond in 1925 for F.G. Simpson whose daughter, Dr Grace Simpson, has given it to the Sackler Library, Oxford. Section XXX, the list of troops in the camp, appears to be incomplete and Dr Brian Dobson made a correct list that is placed at the end of this appendix.

Incpit De Munitionibus Castrorum Liber

I.A. Richmond to F.G. Simpson

My Dear Friend,
Knowing well your constant desire to master the literary side of Roman Archaeology, yet not knowing where any English translation of this book on Castramentation could be obtained, I have tried below to provide you with a translation which may at least serve in the excavator's quarters; and which you may wish to read after Christmastide is over.

Ian A. Richmond
Christmas 1925.

Hygini Gromatici Liber de munitionibus castrorum, INCIPIT

Cap. i.
Now we will demonstrate the tent pitching of the cohorts mentioned above. One tent occupies ten feet, and it receives an additional two feet: It covers eight men. A full century has eighty soldiers; there will be ten tents, which runs to 120 feet in breadth. So far as the thirty-foot breadth of a half-row is concerned ten feet are given to the tent, five to arms, and nine to baggage animals. That makes twenty-four; twice that makes forty-eight. But since the row is sixty feet wide when they are placed together, the remaining twelve feet provide space for communication. This space is based on a full century; out of which sixteen men will be on sentry-go, while each tent will not hold more than eight men. So it comes about that their centurion receives in the same area the space assigned to one of their tents: in other cases it has been necessary to allot more.

Cap. ii.
The legions, as the most faithful provincial troops, ought to go next to the rampart, to guard the work and to enclose within their numbers, like a wall, the tribally requisitioned force. Then when there are additions, when it is necessary to extend the cohort-space, keeping the breadth of the half-row and the same area, we will change it, so that what was 120 x 180 may become 90 x 240, as shown in the diagram, or 60 x 360, as in the large plan. For one cohort occupies 30 x 720 feet: and every time the width is doubled the length is halved. On receiving more legions and fewer auxiliaries, so that it is necessary to place the cohorts round the rampart more frequently, we change the plan. What belonged to the standards goes to the record room, and vice-versa. We change the arrangement of pitching the half-rows, of which we have sub-joined, an instance. Sometimes a cohort gets a space of 150 x 150. But this should be avoided as far as possible, for the centuries will not be able to keep their rows, while one part of the allotted space will be empty, as in the plan below.

Cap. iii
The first cohort, because of the standards and the Eagle, receives a space inside the via sagularis - double because of its double size, as e.g., 120 feet to the standards, 360 to the Record Office, or 180 to the standards and 240 to the Record Office. The arrangement of the area is as the rest. Accordingly, if an odd number of legions, e.g., three, is received, the first two cohorts must pitch along the line of the via sagularis at the side of the praetorium, the other in the praetentura on the left as you enter the porta praetoria, along the line of the via sagularis in the same way. The right hand side must be held by two cohorts from the other units, so that the army can be led out in combination.

Cap iv.
Whenever five or six legions are included, the first two cohorts should pitch at the side of the praetorium, two in the praetentura, beyond which lie the hospitals, then the long-service men or second cohorts: and if the space is cramped, a small infantry cohort may be placed beyond the lines of the long-service men: or if the area is packed tighter still, a legionary cohort should be added, but in order of number. Let the infirmary and other offices beyond it, that is the veterinary hospital and workshop, receive sixty feet, the latter being placed at some distance, so that the infirmary may be quiet for convalescents. The space for these in each kind usually is calculated for 200 men.

Cap. vi.
Long-service legionaries ought to receive the same space as a legionary cohort, because they are calculated at 600 men each. Because of the baggage they ought to pitch in the praetentura, or at the sides of the praetorium, as I had said, beyond the first cohorts. They should not pitch beside the rampart if possible. For the Legate is biased against them: and if the rampart happened to be broken through by the enemy, the legion and its legate would contend that it was done through the long-service men's (negligence).

Cap. vi.
Praetorian cohorts should lie at the sides of the praetorium, and should receive double space, for they use larger tents. The front-rankers and Reserve receive a place in the same area.

Cap. vii.
The Praetorian cavalry lie on the right of the praetorium, the EMPEROR'S Horse Guards on the left. If there is a great number, as for example, 600 Horse Guards and 300 praetorians, 150 Horse Guards could lie in the praetorian lines. So it comes about that they are disposed in equal number, and the Decurions, and other officers who have two horses, may have more space. And if the number of either should be smaller, so that each hundred cavalrymen should space out widely in their half-rows, do not hesitate to assign space there to the nearest officers on the left.

Cap. viii.
If there is received an odd number of praetorian cohorts, while the number and disposition of tents to right and left of the praetorium should be equal, the praetorian cavalry may be put in the place of a cohort. Or if the Horse Guards number eight or nine hundred they should be placed in equal number on both sides with unbroken rows: while if they reach five hundred, half-rows will do for them.

Cap ix.
We must be most careful to see that the side of the praetorium does not exceed 720 feet in length. For so the praetorian cohorts and the rest of the force which pitches at the side of the praetorium best occupy their space with unbroken rows. Then as far as the width of the whole praetorium is concerned from 160 to 220 feet may be observed: in length, as I have said, 720. One must give twenty-five feet to the guards behind the praetorium, or if conditions are cramped, ten feet will be enough.

Cap x.

So to OUR EMPEROR'S Court can be assigned from fifty to seventy feet, in which space the PRAETORIAN PREFECT should be nearest the via principalis. Then, separated by a street, come the praetorian cohorts and the rest of the force. How they should be disposed, we have shown in the book.

Cap xi.

Having set up the altars as in the plan at the end of the book (*Tradition has not preserved this, or the others, which however can be reconstructed from the description - I.A.R.*), we place the Auguratorium on the main street at the right-hand side of the praetorium, so that the General may get the augury properly thereon: the tribunal is placed on the left, so that on receiving the augury he may ascend, and address the troops with favourable omens.

Cap xii.

On the main street, at the middle of the entrance to the praetorium is the point called LOCUS GROMAE, either because the crowd collects there, or because in the laying out of the bounds, when the iron-shod upright has been placed on the spot, the groma is put thereon, that the gates of the camp may form the four quarters in range of the line. And the professional followers of this art are called gromatici for the reason given above.

Cap xiii.

Minor streets should be distributed to run near the via sagularis, so that the lightly armed can make a sally

Cap xiv.

Now I may expound the arrangement of the praetentura. The via principalis, running between the gates to right and left and taking its name from the principia, must be of the same width - that is, 60 feet, as the street between the rampart and the legionaries, which hence is called intervallum. Also the street which leads to the praetorian gate, no doubt so called after the praetorium, must be sixty feet wide as above, because the lines of tents arranged beyond must not project in front of the praetorium, since the standards should look along the via praetoria.

Cap xv.

Then we shall allot a space to the legate on the inside of the main street; this is called the scamnum and has not the ordinary rate of measurement of rows, because of the uncertain numbers of the legions; it should always have a width of fifty to eighty feet, according to these numbers. Here the commandants of the praetorian cohorts usually pitch. A similar position further along should be given to the legionary tribunes, and this also is called the scamnum. There follow, after a street, large or small cavalry regiments, and we have subjoined in the plan how each should be placed after that.

Cap xvi.

Now, to deal with it in its place, as to the large ala. It has twenty four turmae: in these are Decurions, Duplicarii (doubly paid officers), Sesquiplicarii (1 1/2): as many as the numbers of turmae. The decurions keep three horses each, the other officers two. So there are ninety- six more than the thousand, after deducting one for each officer as counting in the thousand. A small ala has sixteen turmae, with decurions and others in accordance and sixty-four horses in excess (*compare above*). So three feet are calculated per man, and nothing taken away. In that area the commandant receives his position, and their higher officers in some cases stretch out, in others receive 2 1/2 feet.

Cap xvii.

So far as the retentura is concerned, the road behind the praetorium, along each side of which, when the force is large, i.e., five legions, usually lie the cohorts of the fifth legion (as those of the third and fourth above in the praetentura) should receive a width of forty feet - or, if there are gates there, fifty, - and is called the quinta because of the forces there.

Cap xviii.
The Quaestorium is so called because the quaestors once were placed there: it lies behind the praetorium in line with the gate, which because the tenth cohorts pitch there, is called the decumana. The quaestorium should be narrower than the praetorium, so that the lines of the guards may be near the back of the praetorium. Here are mostly ambassadors and hostages. And any booty won is placed in the quaestorium.

Cap xix.
At the sides of this building the centuries of the guards should stretch to the via quintana, to hold the rear of the praetorium and to be close to the EMPEROR: to these we will assign double space, because they use the same tents as the praetorians. Behind these should be placed a small cohort, mounted or not, according to the size of the row. In the remaining rows the mounted or un-mounted cohorts should look towards the via quintana, and beyond them should be the newly conquered levies and other tribes. So it comes about that these are enclosed on every side.

Cap xx.
For the via sagularis thirty feet suffices: if there are five legions it should receive a width of forty feet. The scholae, where the daily orders of the legions are posted, should be assigned to the first cohorts opposite the Eagle in the Legate's row.

Cap xxi.
As far as possible the camp should be in the proportion of three to two, so that the breezes may assuage the heat of the army. I have used the word tertiata to mean, for example, 2400 feet long and 1600 feet broad. If the camp is longer, it is called classica naval and the trumpet cannot be heard well at the porta decumana in a tumult. If it is broader, the lay out approaches a square.

Cap xxii.
I think that we have given a sufficiently careful account so far as necessary points are concerned. And henceforward I shall deal with any arrangements, which may become necessary, in their place. Also, so as not to appear to pass over the fortification of camps, the choice of ground in laying them out and the art of avoiding unfavourable positions, I shall deal shortly with them below.

Cap xxiii.
Meanwhile I shall set forth the first steps on laying out, and we may get to know the numbers included by a given shape. Accordingly we shall recapitulate who should be where. At the sides of the praetorium; the preatrorian infantry and cavalry, the IMPERIAL Horse Guards, and large or small alae, if space allows. Beyond the first cohorts, the long-service-men, second cohorts, or small auxiliary cohorts.

Cap xxiv.
Beyond them lie the large or small alae, the Moorish cavalry, and the Pannonian Hussars: all the marines lie forward, because they go out first to make roads and are protected when at work by Moorish cavalry and Pannonian Hussars. Those who should be nearest to the first cohorts are the long service men. So the couriers (speculatores) should be in the row next to the first cohort.

Cap xxv.
In the retentura are the large or small cohorts of mounted infantry, of which I have subjoined the dimensions. All provincial soldiery receives a space of a foot and a fifth, a horseman two and a half and a

fifth. Now to calculate the retentura on receiving the numbers we reduce the mounted infantry in order to assign space to their cohorts more easily.

Cap xxvi.
Thus a large mounted cohort has 240 horsemen, which I reduce to infantry, turning the infantryman's foot into the cavalryman's two and a half feet: this is done by dividing by two and multiplying by five. Treating the 240 horsemen so: 240 becomes 120, and then, multiplies five times, 600. Subtracting the cavalry, there remain 760 men in the cohort, which added to the result above, makes 1360. So we remember that in computing space for a large mounted cohort we must give space for 1360 men.

Cap xxvii.
A small cohort of mounted infantry has the same proportion by half as a large one. The latter has ten centuriae and ten turmae: all have 136 tents, out of which centurions and decurions have one each. A small mounted cohort has six centuries and six turmae: the rest is in half proportion.

Cap xxviii.
A large infantry regiment has ten centuries: it pitches 100 tents, out of which centurions have one each. A small cohort has six centuries, the rest as above.

Cap xix.
Tribal levies - Cantabri, Gaesati, Palmyreni, Daci, Brittones the centuries of the guards, and any additional newly conquered levies allotted to the army, we place in the retentura. To camels with their drivers we assign five feet. If they are to be used in action they should lie in the praetentura next to the marines. If they are to carry booty, next to the quaestorium.

Cap xxx.
Given the numbers written above we calculate as follows.   3 legions, 1500 long-service men, 4 praetrorian cohorts, 400 praetorian cavalry, 450 IMPERIAL Horse Guards, 600 Moorish cavalry, 800 Pannonian Hussars, 500 marines from Misenum, 800 from Ravenna, 320 mounted police (*speculatores. These troops combined police and courier duties, so many were provided by each legion. There was a head office in Rome. I.A.R*), two large cohorts of mounted infantry, for small ones, three large cohorts, three small ones, 500 Palmyreni, 900 Gaesati, 700 Dacians, 500 Britons, 700 Cantabri, two centuries of guards.

Cap xxxi.
Retaining the same numbers, we should make a calculation to know how many half rows there will be in the retentura. The number to go here is 13,640. I take the half, since they pitch in equal proportion, that is 6820. Now let us arrange the sides of the praetorium and calculate in the same way as the retentura, so that we may know what to allot to the legionary cohorts as record-office or standard shrine.

Cap xxxii.
We ought to see that, when three legions with auxiliaries are received, the half of the camp should be 720 feet broad, and at the sides of the camp the cohorts should have 90 feet for records and 240 for standards. So that on deducting the former space and the width of the via sagularis there will remain 600 feet. Let the large alae go to the praetorium according to space: and, in order to allot the remaining space, we fill up one side of the praetorium, to know how many alae will be in the praetentura.

Cap xxxiii.
There are 420 feet vacant for the number of troops at the side of the praetorium. 60 feet go to the praetorium, 20 to the guard, 60 feet to the EMPEROR'S Suite, 40 to the streets, this being almost always the disposition in this breadth. The total is six hundred feet.

Cap xxxiv.
Now to lay out the praetentura, let us compute the number of cavalry remaining. It is 4000, which halved is 2000. A large ala should receive 150 feet for standards, 600 feet for records. On this reckoning 150 feet make five half-rows. A cavalryman receives three feet in a length of 600. I divide by three to know how many fit that length: the result is 200. That will be one half row; now we said five: five times 200 is 1000. That is the space for a large cohort.

Cap xxxv.
We calculate the remaining number, as in the retentura, to know how many half rows there will be. The number, including the space for the hospital, veterinarium and workshop, which are estimated together as 400 men, is 9000. The half is 4500. The half row of the half is 600 feet long, and takes 500 men, as we have said, receiving a foot and one fifth. So it makes no difference whether we make add a fifth to the computed number, or subtract a sixth from the 600 feet. We shall leave 500 as the result, as many men as a row takes.

Cap xxxvi.
If we have 4000 men we see how many we have, that is eight thousand. There will be a corresponding number of half-rows. The result is 240 (i.e. 8 x 30) feet, and we add the 300 feet of the cavalry, computed above: the total is 540 feet. Three cohorts may be put at the side of the praetorium. They make 720 feet, from which is subtracted what the number fills up, 540 feet remain, from (which) may be made six half-rows. As now, a minor street comes beyond the first cohort: that implies four of ten feet each, 40 feet go to streets. 120 feet remain, which we will assign to the lines of the tribunes and Legates, at the rate of 60 feet each.

Cap xxxvii
Now if you order that 1000 men more than the fixed number should be assigned a place in the same area, we proceed as follows. The half of 1000 is 500, the content of one half-row. We subtract ten feet from the officers' quarters and abolish the street given between the cavalry if space permits. 30 feet are thus made, and there will be a half-row to take the additional 500 men.

Cap xxxviii.
Then, as a contrast, let us take away 1000 men, whose area is 60 feet, when the numbers have been made up as before. We shall give 80 feet to the legate's row, 70 to the tribunes, and replace the street between the cavalry.

Cap xxxix.
We observe the same rules at the sides of the praetorium if reduction or amplification is needed - to reduce or enlarge the praetorium, the space for the Suite, and the quaestorium, keeping the proportions of width. If space is crowded streets can be dispensed with between the praetorian infantry and cavalry, since they agree by military discipline each in their own unit, if they observe what I say.

Cap xl.
And in the retentura, those who usually put 500 men in widely or tightly spaced rows, make a more ample pitching than the rows in the given area involve, since it often happens that the numbers have to be changed. Nor can more be abstracted from them than the small cohorts beyond the first legionary cohorts:

and if there is a surplus which does not fill a row, it must be arranged more tightly among the other rows, as I have said. Similarly it is arranged that they shall be spaced out further when the number left is suitable, lest the whole lay-out should be disturbed: and they are pitched with equally wider space throughout the rows of the retentura, when the number thereof has been computed, in agreement with the praetentura.

Cap xli

But if further reduction or enlargement than we have shown is needed, everything is changed, and the cohorts round the ramparts are otherwise arranged.

Cap xlii.

Now we said that the number of half the retentura was 6820, since the width is 600 feet, I see how many half rows there can be: as now there will be 17, and sufficient space (i.e. 90 feet) can be given to the quaestorium. I take the part of the number 17, which is the number of half-rows we said there should be. There are 4000: that will be the number of soldiers; 80 must pitch in one half-row, adding a fifth of a foot. That makes 480 feet. Two cohorts pitch at the side of the retentura.

Cap xliii.

When we distribute the newly-conquered levies and other tribal units in rows, they should not be divided more than thrice nor should they be far separated, so that they may hear one watchword spoken in their own tongue. We must see to assign the same space to the standards of the first block as to those of the first cohort, so that the minor streets may run past them.

Cap xliiii

So there will be 16 cohorts on the sides: 4000 are in the praetorium and retentura: and each have 60 x 360 feet. The remaining 4000 are inside the via sagularis.

Cap xlv.

According to my ability, MY LORD BROTHER, I have perused all the authors in brief, and whatever they have laid down about making summer-camps I have stated in arrangement in this book, before setting forth the numbers. To this day no author in dealing with the first stages of camp layout has explained the fundamentals, and so I hope that our care in the matter may merit YOUR pleasure.

Cap xlvi.

Thus we have set forth the types of units and placed a whole army in position. We have even shown what number should be changed if need arise. For that cavalry should be placed in the retentura and the infantry without mounted detachments in the praetentura, except under compulsion, is an unquestionable sign of in experience in the surveyor. If there is no mounted infantry in the army, it can obviously be seen that we place small alae on the sides of the quaestorium, so that the retentura may have some cavalry.

Cap xlviii. Cap xlvii

As for the legions and the bisection, which demonstrate the difficulties even of experts in castramentation, I have elaborated especially carefully the method of lay-out which I have invented in connexion with the numbers of centuries; so that if YOU would deign to allow it, I might be the first to bring this novelty in measurement to YOUR MAGNITUDE, which I hope will please YOU, if YOU will first investigate the measurement in daily use.

Now let us briefly run through the fortifications and similar matters, on which many authors have written. The fortification of summer-camps is effected in five methods: ditch, rampart; "stag-horns"; arms; bank.

Cap xlvix.
The ditch is made in a secure position for the sake of discipline, and is of a "gabled" or Punic type. It is called gabled when it has sides carried down from the top and is joined at the bottom. When the outer side is perpendicular, it is called Punic, the opposite side being carried down as in the gabled type. Both should have a minimum width of five feet and depth of three. Sixty feet outside, for the width of the gates, a ditch is made in the same way; this is called a titulus (a label) because of its shortness.

Cap l.
In a less secure position a rampart should be constructed with turves or stones, rock or rough stone. Eight feet wide and six feet high is enough. And a small breastwork is made at the titulus in front of the gates in the same way as the rampart at the ditch. This is called holy because of its position.   (*Gates and boundaries were holy: cf. Romulus and Remus, I.A.R.*)

Cap li.
"Stag horns" are forked stakes. One takes refuge in these if the sod breaks with excessive friability by nature of the soil, or if the rampart cannot be built with shifting stone except under pressure, or if the ditch cannot be made without side-slips.

Cap lii.
Where there are no "stag-horns" and the position is somewhat unsafe, they fortify camps with four rows of armed men, so that sentinels are posted at more frequent intervals in each row. In peacetime one row of armed men suffices for discipline, and the sentinels are less closely packed.

Cap liii.
The rampart is made with heaped material if the position is rocky or sandy, which indubitably offers a fortification to a camp when the heap is made.

Cap liv.
The angles of the camp should be curved, for they complete the corners and strengthen and leave attackers exposed. They should be described from the angle of the cohorts, which make a radius of 60 feet, as far as includes the outer lines, which describe a quarter circle.

Cap lv.
A clavicle is set out similarly from the inner line of the rampart, the centre being the middle of the gate and the compass being extended to the hinge thereof. From this centre make a circle at the other side of the road with the same line, which will serve as a centre, add the width of the rampart and scribe in the same line. So may those who enter always be discovered: while these devices exclude anyone approaching in direct line. The clavicula takes its name from its action.

Cap lvi.
So far as the choice of ground in determining the layout is concerned, that position is considered first class which rises gently to a height from the lain: in such a position the Porta Decumana is fixed at the highest point, so that the different parts of the camp may lie beneath it. The Porta Preatoria should always face the enemy. The position considered second class is level; third class on a hill; fourth class on a mountain; fifth class in an unavoidable position - whence the term "necessary camp".

Cap lvii.
Particular watch should be kept on a road which overlooks the sides of a camp. Also at one or other side in any position it should have a river or spring. Bad positions, which our ancestors called "step mothers", should be avoided anyhow! A hill over which enemy may come or spy what is going on in the camp

should not dominate it. Nor should a wood providing concealment lie near, nor gullies nor valleys whence the enemy may creep up onto the camp. See that spates in an adjacent river do not destroy the camp in a sudden storm.

Cap lviii
One must remember to make double and frequent ramps up to the rampart on the enemies' side, and to build platforms for artillery round the gates and at angles, in place of towers. The rampart will be fitted out with most artillery on that side where "step mothers" are, if they cannot be avoided! EXPLICIT LIBER DE MUNITIONIBVS CASTRORUM FELCITER. ANN DN MIMXXV.

FINIS

A SHORT COMMENTARY ON THE DATE AND AUTHORSHIP OF THE TREATISE

The age, authorship and original title of the treatise on castramentation are matters of doubt. It has been claimed, notably by Lange, that it was written about the opening of the second century by C. Iulius Hyginus, an evocatus Augusti employed as surveyor in Trajan's reign [1] and that its title was *Liber de munitionubus castrorum*. Yet the red superscript INCIPIT LIBER HYGINI GROMATICI, which gives the book its title was added to the sixth century codex Arcerianus {Wolfenbuttel 36-23}, during its sojourn at Bobbio, in the ninth century: and it precedes not the text under present consideration, but a small mathematical fragment which, thus transposed, takes the place of the missing portion of the text. The subscript is LIBER GROMATICUS -- HYGINI DE DIVISIONIB AGRORV EXPLICIT. As Lange points out, this description is probably to be explained by the unfortunate habit of making the superscript precede the subscript at the junction of two books. [2] But it tells us nothing about the title or author of our text.

It is possible, however, that a second group of manuscripts, derived from the lost codex Gaetesianus, embodies sound tradition. There are two types of superscript; a) cod. Guelferbytanus C {Wolfenbuttel 36-23 saec. Xvi} HYGINI GROMATICI LIBER. The subscript, LIBER GROMATICUS HYGINI DE MUNITIONIBUS CASTRORUM EXPLICIT, is common to both, but B drops the H. Yet if a critic were to suggest that these were divergent emendations of original titles mutilated or displaced, as were those of the codex Arcerianus, what satisfactory contradiction would be made?

If the tradition discussed in the last paragraph is genuine, the author may be identified as C. Iulius Hyginus, who assigned lands in Pannonia to veterans in Trajan's reign. But internal evidence suggests that the book was not quite so early as this. That it does not mention the equites legionis has been pointed out already by von Domaszewski. This is an odd omission, but is valueless for dating, since inscriptions prove that these cavalrymen continued part of the army as long as the Praetorians, who are prominently mentioned. In fact it is the non Roman Palmyreni and Brittones who provide termini. Of the former the last epigraphical record belongs to the time of Gordian III, (AD 238), and, since they were always recruited therefrom, they cannot have lasted after the ruin of their community thirty-five years later. The Britons belong to that class of levy which appears for the first time under Trajan, represented then by the Mauri Equites of Lusius Quietus: and we know the first appearance of these British units coincides with the Caledonian activity of Antonius Pius in AD 142-5 and with the organisation of the German frontier at that time. Nor can the (Raeti) Gaesati, who appear only in the Antonine fort at High Rochester (Bremenium) be much earlier in date. The book therefore falls within a period later than Trajan's reign, if

---
[1] This comes from a book indubitably his, *De divisionibus agrorum*.
[2] e.g, algebraically the relation would be thus between books A,B,C,D. A' - B'A2-C'B2-D'C2-D2.

this interpretation of internal evidence is correct. And in the absence of the opening chapters, which no doubt would have given the precise indication needed, this is perhaps as far as we dare safely tread; with an inclination towards an earlier date in view of the simple Imperial titles.

Apart from questions of date and authorship it should be noted that the method of mensuration described in the treatise is not that in daily use in the Roman army; it is meant to be an improvement thereon. Nor is the force such as would be all in use at any one time. If the camel corps induces an oriental atmosphere, the Raeti Gaesati tell us of the stinging northwestern cold. The same thing is true of the mixture of irregulars and marines, Moorish light horse and Pannonian Hussars. Such an army in fact reproduces the motley of the chess board; the combination is ludicrous, yet the units are each true to type, and the constitution of each one is correct. For is the game not meant to prepare the mind for sterner warfare?

I.A. Richmond

Dr Brian Dobson's translation of Cap xxx
Three legions, 1600 vexillarii, 4 cohortes praetoriae, 400 praetorian cavalry, 450 equites singulars imperotis, 4 alae milliariae, 5 alae quingenariae, 600 Mauri equites, 800 Pannonian veredarii, 500 Misenum fleet, 800 Ravenna fleet, 200 scouts, 2 cohortes equitatae milliariae, 4 equitatae quingenariae, 3 cohortes peditatae milliariae, 3 cohortes quingenariae, 500 Palmyrenes, 900 Gaetuli, 500 Brittones, 700 Cantabri, 2 centuries of statores.

APPENDIX TWO

SOME ROMAN CAMPS IN BRITAIN

The following list has been extracted from the literature but is by no means a complete inventory. The area R is in *a.q.* computed at the rampart's inner face; Asp R is the aspect ratio. The estimates of notional cohorts (N) are the best possible, given the plan scales and are reported as calculated. Some of these will be slight over-estimates where the dimensions were taken from ditch crop-marks which lie several feet outside the inner face of the rampart.

Camp	Asp R		R	N	Data source
Grindon School	1	1	1.0	0.30	Welfare & Swan (1995)
Coesike E	7	8	1.7	0.50	"
Grindon Hill *	1	1	1.1	0.50	"
Warcop	2	3	1.9	0.60	"
Coesike W1	1	1	2.0	0.64	"
Bowes Moor	1	1	2.6	0.75	"
Swine Hill 2	1	1	2.6	0.82	"
Brown Dikes	1	1	3.75	1.1	Welfare & Swan (1995)
Sunny Rigg 1	2	3	3.4	1.1	"
Nowtler Hill 1	7	8	3.8	1.2	"
Walwick Fell	1	1	4.5	1.4	"
Willowford	3	4	4.5	1.4	"
Golden Fleece	4	5	4.5	1.5	"
Sunny Rigg 2	4	5	4.7	1.5	"
Chapel Rigg	4	5	4.9	1.6	"
Cawfields	4	5	4.9	1.6	"
Troutbeck 3	1	1	5.0	1.6	"
Haltwhistle Burn 2	1	2	5.2	1.7	"
Moss Side 1	1	2	5.3	1.7	"
Barrockside*	2	3	5.8	1.8	"
Langwathby	7	8	6.6	2.1	Welfare & Swan (1995)
Ardoch 6	3	5	7.2	2.2	St Joseph (1969)
Bootham Stray 1	1	2	7.6	2.3	Welfare & Swan (1995)
Crooks	2	3	7.3	2.3	"
Haltwhistle Burn 1	1	2	7.8	2.4	"
Broomby La 2	1	2	7.8	2.4	"
Glenwhelt Leazes	1	2	8.9	2.8	"
Cow Dykes	1	1	9.0	2.9	Villy (1912)[1] see end note
Quatt	2	3	9.6	3.1	Welfare & Swan (1995)
Kirkby Thore 3	6	7	10.7	3.4	"
Markham Cot 2	4	5	10.4	3.3	"
Cawthorn D	5	6	10.7	3.4	"
Greenlee Lough	4	5	11.2	3.6	"
Farnley 3	2	3	11.9	3.8	"
Twice Brewed	2	3	11.9	3.8	"
Knowe Farm	4	5	12.0	3.8	"
Lees Hall	2	3	12.8	4.0	Welfare & Swan (1995)
Ardoch 1	11	12	13.0	4.2	St Joseph (1969)
K. Thore 2	2	3	13.5	4.3	Welfare & Swan (1995)
Burnswark N	1	4	16.1	4.3	Keppie (1984)
Sills Burn N	5	6	14.0	4.5	Welfare & Swan (1995)
Sills Burn S	2	5	15.3	4.6	"

Camp	Asp R		R	N	Data source
Cawthorn C	1	3	16.3	4.7	Welfare & Swan (1995)
Woodhead	1	2	15.9	4.9	Maxwell (1983)
N Yardhope	20	21	15.6	5.0	Welfare & Swan (1995)
Cawthorn A	1	1	17.9	5.7	"
Broomby La 1	5	6	18.6	5.9	"
Cawthorn B	5	6	18.8	6.0	Welfare & Swan (1995)
Chew Green 4	10	11	18.8	6.0	"
Swine Hill 1	15	16	19.0	6.1	"
Burlington 2	2	3	20.0	6.7	"
Birdhope 2	10	11	24.1	7.7	Welfare & Swan (1995)
Gleadthorpe	4	5	25.4	8.1	"
Dun	4	5	25.7	8.2	St Joseph (1973)
Bagraw S	2	3	26.0	8.2	Welfare & Swan (1995)
Seatsides 2	2	3	26.8	8.5	"
Burnhead	2	3	27.7	8.8	"
Farnsfield	7	8	27.8	8.9	"
Bagraw N	2	3	28.5	9.0	Welfare & Swan (1995)
Moss Side 2	10	11	30.5	9.8	"
Ardoch 2	9	10	30.6	9.8	St Joseph (1969)
Troutbeck 1	10	11	31.2	10.0	Welfare & Swan (1995)
Milrighall	1	1	31.2	10.0	Maxwell & Wilson (1987)
Wath	13	14	38.2	12.2	Welfare & Swan (1995)
Kirkby Thore 1	4	5	38.4	12.3	"
Ardoch 3	5	6	39.8	12.7	St Joseph (1969)
Burnswark S	4	5	39.7	12.7	Keppie (1986)
Chew Green 3	2	3	41.9	13.2	Welfare & Swan (1995)
Dargues	2	3	46.3	14.6	"
Esgairperfedd	9	10	47.4	15.2	St Joseph (1969)
Ardoch 4	14	15	47.6	15.3	"
Milestone House	1	2	52.3	16.1	Welfare & Swan (1995)
Seatsides 1	10	11	53.8	17.2	"
St Harmon	2	3	55.4	17.5	St Joseph (1969)
Fell End	2	3	60.0	19.0	Welfare & Swan (1995)
Rey Cross	1	1	62.4	20.0	Welfare & Swan (1995)
Chew Green 1	1	1	60.8	20.1	"
Malham	6	7	63.3	20.3	"
Horstead	2	3	66.7	21.1	"
Bromfield	4	5	69.3	22.1	"
Walford	2	3	74.9	23.7	"
Crackenthorpe	1	1	75.0	24.0	"
Inchtuthil camp	3	5	77.3	24.2	St Joseph (1973)
Mentieth	3	5	77.3	24.2	"
Dalginross	1	1	80.0	25.6	Collingwood & Richmond (1969)
Ancaster	2	3	89.3	27.3	Welfare & Swan (1995)
W Woodburn	6	7	90.6	28.9	"

Camp	Asp R		R	N	Data source
Birdhope 1	5	6	96.5	30.9	Welfare & Swan (1995)
E Learmouth	2	3	101.3	32.0	"
Norton 1	2	3	101.4	32.0	"
Greensforge 5	3	4	104.9	33.4	"
Caerau	8	9	107.7	34.5	St Joseph (1969)
Stracathro	5	6	117.5	37.5	St Joseph (1958)
Swindon	2	3	121.0	38.2	Welfare & Swan (1995)
Burlington 1	3	4	122.2	38.4	"
Featherwood W	2	3	125.8	39.7	"
Uffington 2	2	3	125.4	39.7	"
Featherwood E	1	1	125.5	40.2	"
Bellshiel	2	3	128.7	40.7	"
Troutbeck 2	6	7	128.6	41.1	"
Markham Cot 1	4	5	129.8	41.4	"
Silloans	2	3	137.7	43.5	"
Uffington 1	2	3	143.5	45.3	"
Cleghorn	2	3	144.6	45.8	Keppie (1986)
Brampton Bryan	5	6	195.8	62.5	Welfare & Swan (1995)
Ardoch 5	2	3	204.5	64.7	St Joseph (1977)
Rae Dykes	5	6	299.7	95.7	Collingwood & Richmond (1969)
Dunning	1	1	248.4	111.5	St Joseph (1973)
Abernethy	11	12	360.6	116.0	St Joseph (1973)
Ardoch 7	2	3	394.5	124.6	St Joseph 1977
Durno	2	3	450.4	142.5	St Joseph 1977
Newstead	5	6	455.8	145.9	"
St Leonard's	4	5	498.3	199.4	"

[1] Villy described a perfect example of a parallelogram-shaped Roman camp with sides of three *actus* but, following the fashionable scepticism of the time, strained every argument to refute its Roman origin. The author found a piece of Roman pottery on the site, kindly confirmed by Mr Percival Turnbull.

APPENDIX THREE

AN ALGORITHM FOR MILITARY GRANARIES

It is possible to construct a simple spreadsheet to give possible options for granaries of known area. The model presumes an input of 50 *modii* for each sq. foot of floor area and an annual consumption of 48 *modii* per infantryman, after a 4% volume loss. This loss is not built into the cavalry granary because they were regularly replenished, so each auxiliary cavalryman took 456 *modii*.

Take the area (A) within the walls in Roman feet and multiply by 10 to give the volume of grain (V) in *modii*. (V x 0.96) / (48/52) is the number of the infantry man-weeks of corn (C); multiplying V by 0.96 accounts for the 4% loss in storage. For the auxiliary cavalry, the corresponding value (K) is V / (452/52). Dividing C and K by W weeks will give the number of men it will feed in that period. Likewise dividing C by the number of men (M) will give the number of weeks that the corn will last. For a two floored granary the results are simply doubled. Table A3.1 shows the spreadsheet.

TABLE A3.1

SPREADSHEET FOR GRANARY OPTIONS

(In-puts in bold type)

Granary area	**(A)**			
	1 floor		2 floors	
Storage volume	(V = A x 50) modii		(2 V)	
	Infantry (S)	Cavalry (H)	Infantry (S)	(H) cavalry
Men-weeks	C = V x 0.96 x (48/52)	K = (456 / 52)	2C	2K
	Men		Men	
No of weeks (**W**)	C / W	K / W	2 (C / W)	2 (K/W)
	Weeks		Weeks	
No of men (**M**)	C / M	K / M	2 (C / M)	2 (K/M)

Table A3.2 shows a spreadsheet for the Stanwix granary, which almost certainly covered 3,800 sq. feet (36.58 m. x 9.14 m.; Gentry 1976). It indicates that with two floors, the corn would last 720 cavalry 12 weeks. The plausibility of these figures is supported by the last value being a whole number to the first decimal place.

TABLE A3.2

SPREADSHEET FOR OPTIONS FOR THE STANWIX FORT GRANARY

(In-puts in bold type.)

Granary area (sq. ft.)	**3800**			
Storage volume (modii.)	1 floor 38,000		2 floors 76,000	
	Infantry (S)	Cavalry (H)	Infantry (S)	(H) cavalry
Men-weeks	39,250	4,333	79,040	8,667
No of weeks	men		men	
1	39,250	4333	79,040	8,667
52	760	83	1,520	167
No of men	weeks		weeks	
60	659	72.2	1,317	144
720	55	6.02	110	12.04

****

BIBLIOGRAPHY

1. BELLHOUSE, R.L., & RICHARDSON G.G.S., 1982: *The Trajanic fort at Kirkbride: the terminus of the Stanegate frontier,* Transactions of the Cumberland & Westmorland Antiquarian & Archaeological Society (2nd Series), 82, 35-50.
2. BIDWELL, P., 1999: Hadrian's Wall 1989-1999, Cumberland & Westmorland Antiquarian & Archaeological Society and the Society of Antiquaries of Newcastle upon Tyne.
3. BIRLEY, E., 1958: *The Roman fort at Brough under Stainmore,* Transactions of the Cumberland & Westmorland Antiquarian & Archaeological Society (2nd Series), 58, 31-62.
4. BIRLEY, E., 1957: *The Roman fort at Watercrook,* Transactions of the Cumberland & Westmorland Antiquarian & Archaeological Society, 57 (2nd Series), 12-18.
5. BIRLEY, E., 1963: *Roman Papcastle,* Transactions of the Cumberland & Westmorland Antiquarian & Archaeological Society, (2nd Series), 63, 96-125.
6. BIRLEY, R., 1976: *Vindolanda,* 33, (London, Thames & Hudson).
7. BREEZE, D.J. and DOBSON B. 2000: *Hadrian's Wall,* (Penguin).
8. BUCKLAND, P., 1978: *A first century shield from Doncaster,* Britannia IX, 247-270.
9. CAMPBELL, B., 2000: *The writings of the Roman land surveyors. Introduction, Text and Commentary,* Journal of Roman Studies, monograph no 9, London.
10. COLLINGWOOD, R.G., 1922: *The Roman fort at Lyne, Peeblesshire,* Transactions of the Cumberland & Westmorland Antiquarian & Archaeological Society (2nd Series), 22, 169-185.
11. COLLINGWOOD, R.G., 1928: *Hardknott Castle,* Transactions of the Cumberland & Westmorland Antiquarian & Archaeological Society (2nd Series), 28, 314-352.
12. COLLINGWOOD, R.G., & RICHMOND, I.A., 1969: *The Archaeology of Roman Britain,* (London, Methuen).
13. COLLINGWOOD BRUCE, J., 1966: *Handbook to the Roman Wall,* 12th Edition, edited by Sir Ian Richmond, (Newcastle, Hindson and Andrew Reid).
14. Crofton A., 1885: *The Mickle Ditch,* Lancashire and Cheshire Antiquarian Society, vol. 3, 190.
15. CRUMMY, P., 1982: *The origin of some major Romano British towns,* Britannia, III, 125 – 135.
16. CRUMMY, P., 1985: *Colchester: the mechanics of laying out a town,* in *Roman urban topography in Britain and the western empire,* CBA Research Report.
17. DACRE, J.A., 1985: *An Excavation on the Roman fort at Stanwix, Carlisle,* Transactions of the Cumberland & Westmorland Antiquarian & Archaeological Society (2nd Series), 85, 53-69.
18. DILKE, O.A.W.. 1971: *The Roman Land Surveyors: An Introduction to the Agrimensores,* (Newton Abbot, David & Charles).
19. DILKE, O.A.W., 1987: *Mathematics and Measurement,* (London, British Museum Publications).
20. EDWARDS B.J.N., 2000: *The Romans at Ribchester,* (CNWRS, University of Lancaster) 44-45.
21. EVANS, J. & SCULL, C., 1990: *Fieldwork at the Roman site at Blennerhasset, Cumbria,* Transactions of the Cumberland & Westmorland Antiquarian & Archaeological Society (2nd Series), 90, 127-138.
22. FERRAR M.J. & RICHARDSON, A., 2003: *The Roman Survey of Britain,* British Archaeological Reports, Series 359.
23. FRERE, S.S., HASSAL, M.W.C. & TOMLIN, R.S.O., 1977: *Roman Britain in 1976,* Britannia, VIII, 356-425.
24. FRERE, S.S., HASSAL, M.W.C. & TOMLIN, R.S.O., 1985: *Roman Britain in 1984,* Britannia, XVI, 253.
25. FRERE, S.S., 1987: *Roman Britain in 1986,* Britannia, XVIII, 301-376.

26. FRERE, S.S., HASSAL, M.W.C. & TOMLIN, R.S.O., 1989: *Britain in 1988*, Britannia, XVIX, 259 -345.
27. GOODBURN, R., 1979: *Roman Britain in 1978*, Britannia, X, 325.
28. HANDFORD, S.A., 1951: *Caesar: the Conquest of Gaul*, London, Penguin.
29. HANDFORD, S.A., 1963: *Sallust: The Jugurthine War / The Conspiracy of Catiline*, London, Penguin.
30. HANSON, W.S., 1977-8: Roman campaigns north of the Forth-Clyde isthmus: The Evidence of Temporary Camps, *Proceedings of the Society of Antiquaries of Scotland*, 109, 140-150.
31. HART, C.R., 1984: *The North Derbyshire Archaeological Survey to AD 1500*, Derbyshire Archaeological Society, 90.
32. HARTLEY, B. R., 1987: *Roman Ilkley*, Olicana Museum and Historical Society, Ilkley.
33. HAVERFIELD, F., 1920: *Old Carlisle*, Transactions of the Cumberland & Westmorland Antiquarian & Archaeological Society (2nd Series), 20, 143-150.
34. HEATH, T., 1921: *A History of Greek Mathematics*; Oxford, Clarendon Press.
35. HILDYARD, E.J.W., 1954: *Excavations at Burrow in Lonsdale*, Transactions of the Cumberland & Westmorland Antiquarian & Archaeological Society (2nd Series), 54, 86
36. JOHNSON, A., 1983: *Roman Forts*, (London, Adam & Charles Black).
37. JOHNSON, S., 1978: *Excavations at Hayton near York*, Britannia, IX, 57-114.
38. KEPPIE, L., 1984: *The Making of the Roman Army from Republic to Empire*, (London, Batsford.)
39. KEPPIE, L., 1986: *Scotland's Roman Remains*, (Edinburgh, John Donald).
40. JONES, G.B.D., 1968: *Romans in the Northwest*, in Northern History, 3, 1-26.
41. JONES, G.B.D. & GREALEY, S., 1974: *Roman Manchester*, Manchester University Press.
42. MACDONALD, G., 1934: *The Roman Wall in Scotland*, Oxford, Clarendon Press.
43. MAXWELL, G.S., 1983: *Recent aerial discoveries in Roman Scotland, Drumquassle, Eliginhaugh and Woodhead*, Britannia, XIII, 167-183.
44. MAXWELL, G.S. & WILSON, D.R., 1987: *Air Reconnaissance in Roman Britain, 1977 - 84*, Britannia, XVIII, 1 - 48.
45. MILNER, N.P., 1993: *Vegetius: Epitome of Military Science*, Liverpool University Press.
46. MOLLWEIDE, 1813: Quoted by Cantor (1875, 68-69) and cited by Dilke 1971.
47. PEDDIE, J., 1996-7: *The Roman War Machine*, (Stroud, Sutton).
48. PHILLIPS, B.J., 1977: *The forum of Roman London*, Britannia, VIII, 1-64.
49. PHILPOTT, R. A., 1998: *New evidence from aerial reconnaissance for Roman military sites in Cheshire*, Britannia, XXIX, 341-356.
50. POULTER A., 1982: *Old Penrith: Excavations in 1977 and 1979*, Transactions of the Cumberland & Westmorland Antiquarian & Archaeological Society (2nd Series), 82, 51 – 66.
51. RAMSEY, W. & LANCIANI, R.., 1901: *A Manual of Roman Antiquities*, (London, Charles Griffin & Co.)
52. RODWELL, W., 1972: *The Roman fort at Great Chesterford*, Britannia, II, 290-293.
53. RICHARDSON, A., 1997: *Observations of the Geometry of Roman Camps*, Transactions of the Cumberland & Westmorland Antiquarian & Archaeological Society (2nd Series), 97, 45-55.
54. RICHARDSON, A., 2000: *The Numerical Basis of Roman Camps*, Oxford Journal of Archaeology, Vol. 19, No. 4, 425-437.
55. RICHARDSON, A., 2001: *The Order of Battle in the Roman Army: Evidence from Marching Camps*, Oxford Journal of Archaeology, Vol. 20, No.2, 171-185.
56. RICHARDSON, A., 2002: *Camps and Forts of Units and Formations of the Roman army*, Oxford Journal of Archaeology, Vol. 21, No 1, 93-107.
57. RICHARDSON, A., 2003: *Space and manpower in Roman camps*, Oxford Journal of Archaeology, Vol. 22 (3), 303-313.

58. RICHARDSON, A., 2003b: *The possible historic contexts of some Roman camps in Cumberland*, Transactions of the Cumberland & Westmorland Antiquarian & Archaeological Society (3rd Series), 3, 91-96.
59. RICHARDSON, A., 2004: *Granaries and Garrisons in Roman Forts*, Oxford Journal of Archaeology, Vol. 23, 4, 429 - 442.
60. RICHMOND, I. A., 1925: Hyginus, *De Munitionibus Castrorum*, a manuscript translation now in the Sackler Library, Oxford.
61. RICHMOND, I. A., 1962: *The Roman Siege Works at Masada, Israel*, Journal of Roman Studies, 52, 1142-155.
62. ST. JOSEPH, J.K., 1958: *Air Reconnaissance in Britain, 1955-1957*, Journal of Roman Studies, 48, 86 -101.
63. ST. JOSEPH, J.K., 1969: *Air Reconnaissance in Britain, 1965-1968*, Journal of Roman Studies, 59, 102-128.
64. ST. JOSEPH, J.K., 1973: *Air Reconnaissance in Britain, 1969-1972*, Journal of Roman Studies, 63, 214-246.
65. ST. JOSEPH, J.K., 1977: *Air Reconnaissance in Britain, 1973-1976*, Journal of Roman Studies, 67, 125-161.
66. SAUER, E., 2001: *Roman Alchester*, Current Archaeology, 173, 189-191.
67. SCHULTEN, A., 1933: *Geschichte von Numantia* (Munchen), cited by Keppie (1984).
68. SCOTT-KILVERT, I., 1979: *Polybius: The Rise of the Roman Empire*, (London, Penguin).
69. SHOTTER, D. & WHITE, A., 1995: *The Romans in Lunesdale*, (CNWRS, University of Lancaster) 21.
70. SIMPSON, F.G. & RICHMOND, I.A., 1936: *The Roman fort on the Stanegate, and other remains, at Old Church Brampton*, Transactions of the Cumberland & Westmorland Antiquarian & Archaeological Society (2nd Series), 36, 172-182.
71. START, D., 1985: *The Roman fort at Castle Shaw*, Greater Manchester Archaeology J. Vol. 1, 13-18.
72. TODD, M., 1985: *The Roman fort at Bury Barton, Devonshire*, Britannia XVI, 49-55.
73. VILLY, F., 1912: *A Supposed Roman camp near Harrogate*, Yorkshire Archaeological Journal. Vol. 12, 145 – 149.
74. VON DOMASZCEWSKI, A., 1967: *Die Rangordnung des romiches Heeres*, Cologne, 35.
75. WEBSTER, G., 1969: *The Roman Imperial Army*, (London, Constable).
76. WELFARE, H. & SWAN V., 1995: *Roman camps in England: The Field Archaeology*, Royal Commission on Historic Monuments, (London, HMSO).
77. WELLESLEY, K., 1964: *Tacitus: The Histories*, (London, Penguin).
78. WILLIAMSON, G.A., 1959: *Josephus : The Jewish War*, (London, Penguin).
79. WILSON, D.R., 1972: *Roman Britain in 1971*: Britannia, III, 299-367.
80. WILSON, D.R., WRIGHT, R.D. & HASSAL, M.W.C., 1973: *Roman Britain in 1972*: Britannia, IV, 290.
81. WILSON, D.R., 1974: *Roman Britain in 1973*, Britannia, V, 399.
82. ZANT, J.M., 2001: *An excavation at Brougham Castle*, Transactions of the Cumberland & Westmorland Antiquarian & Archaeological Society, (3rd series) 1, 31-43.

INDEX

A

Abernethy, 22, 81
actus, definition of, 8
Agricola, Julius, 59
agrimensores, 8, 32, 67
Ala Augusta Vocontiorum civium Romanorum, 44
Ala II Flavia pia fidelis milliaria, 43
Ala Petriana, 43, 44
Ala quingenaria, 25, 29, 39, 40, 41, 42, 47, 57, 58, 61, 75
    forts for, 39, 40
Ala milliaria, 25, 29, 37, 41, 42, 58, 61, 74
    forts for, 41, 43-45
Albinus, Aulus, 56
Alchester, 41
Alesia, 67
Alexander, the Great, 4
Ambleside, 38
Ancaster, 80
Antonine Wall, 51, 54
Antoninus Pius, emperor, 77
Arcerianus, codex, 77
Archytas of Tara, 21
Ardoch, 22, 40, 64, 65, 79, 80, 81
Army, Roman,
    battle order, 55-60, 64
    consular, 11, 12, 13, 14, 15, 60
    imperial, 25-28
    rations, 49
    Spain, in, 16-19
arithmetic mean, 21
aspect ratios of camps, 21-24
    calculations for, 24
auguratorium, 71

B

Bagraw, South, 60, 80
Balmackewan, 64, 65
Balmuidy, 54
Bannaventa, 42
Bar Hill, 54
Barochan Hill, 38
barracks,
    at Fendoch, 35, 36
    at Renieblas 17-19, 28
Barrockside, 79
Bavaria, 52
Bearsden, 54
Beckfoot, 62
Bede, Venerable, 55
Bellshiel, 61, 81
Benwell, 51, 53, 62
Bewcastle, 51, 53, 62
Birdhope, 80, 81
Birdoswald, 51, 52, 53, 62
Birrens, 39
Blennerhasset, 41
Bobbio, 77
Bonnytown, 64
Bootham Stray, 79
booty, 72, 73
Bowes Moor, 58, 79
Bowness on Solway, 51, 52, 53, 62
Bothwellhaugh, 40
Brampton Bryan, 59, 81
Brampton, Old Church, 38, 61
Brinno, 48
Brittones, 29, 73, 77
Bromfield, 80
Broomby Lane, 79, 80
Brougham, 39
Brough on Noe, 38
Brough under Stainmore, 38
Brown Dykes, 58, 79
Buckton Park, 40
Burgh by Sands, 52, 53, 62
Burlington, 61, 80, 81
Burnhead, 80
Burnswark, 56, 79, 80
Burrow in Lonsdale, 40
Bury Barton, 38

C

Caceres, 13, 19
Cadder, 54
Caerau, 38, 39, 45, 61, 81
Caerhun, 39
Caerleon, 46
Caesar, Julius, 67
Calverton, 58
camels, 73
Camp, Roman,
    acreage to notional cohorts, 30
    aspect ratios of, 21-24
    early plan, 4-7
    emperor's suite, 30, 31
    Hyginian, 26-31, 37, App. 1
    legionary, examples of, 31

number and distribution in England, 55
outlines of camps, 16, 21-22
orientation of, 32
Polybian, 12-13, 30
site, choice of, 32, 76
space, partition, of, 32
Cantabri, 29, 73
Cardean, 64, 65
Carpow, 41
Carrawborough, 51, 52, 53, 62
Carriden, 54
Carvoran, 51, 52, 53, 62
Carzield, 40
Castillejo, 16, 19
Castlecary, 54
Castledykes, 64
Castlesteads, 51, 52, 53, 62
Castle Shaw, 38, 45
Catterick, 41
cavalry, 7,
    legionary, 29
    auxiliary officers, 71
Caves Inn, 39
Cawfields, 79
Cawthorn C, 23, 38, 79, 80
centuriation, 8
century, 3
    theoretical camps for, 7
Chapel Rigg, 79
Chester, 46
Chesters, 51, 52, 53, 62
Chesters, Great, 51, 52, 53, 62
Chesterford, Great, 42, 46
Chew Green, 60, 80
Christianity, 32
Civilis, Julius, 48
classica naval, 23, 72
Claudius, emperor, 55
claviculae, 21, 76
Cleghorn, 81
Clifford, 41
Coesike E & W, 58, 79
Cohors I Hamiorum Sagittarium, 52
Cohors II Tungorum equitata, 52
Cohors IV Gallorum equitata, 52
cohors peditata quingenaria, 25, 27, 28, 29, 35, 36, 38, 39, 42, 47, 52, 57, 58, 61, 62
    forts for, 38, 39
cohors peditata milliaria, 25, 27, 28, 29, 42, 47, 52, 58, 61, 73
    forts for, 39
cohors equitata quingenaria, 25, 27, 28, 29, 35, 36, 39, 40, 41, 42, 47, 52, 57, 58, 61, 73
    forts for, 39

cohors equitata milliaria, 25, 27, 28, 29, 35, 39, 42, 47, 52, 58, 61, 73
    forts for, 40, 41
cohorts, legionary, 25, 27, 28, 70
Colchester, 46
Corpus Agrimensorum Romanorum, 33
Cow Dykes, 79
Crackenthorpe, 61, 80
Cramond, 40
Crooks, 79
Cumbria, 55, 61,
    coastal forts, 62

D

Daci, 73
Dalginross, 64, 80
Dargues, 80
De munitionibus castrorum, 3, 25, see Appendix One,
decempedae, 9
decumanus, 8, 57
Defence,
    of camps, 76
    of forts, 47, 48
Dere Street, 55
Devon 55
ditches, 47, 76
Dobson, Dr Brian, 78
Dornoch, 64
Drumburgh, 52, 53
Drumlanrigg, 39
Drumquassle, 38
Dun, 60, 80
Dunblane, 64
Dunning, 64, 81
Durham, Co., 55
Durno, 64, 81

E

Eden, River, 61
Elginhaugh, 38
Epirus, 4
Esgairperfedd, 80
Essex, 55
Etruscans, 7
Exeter, 46

F

Farnley, 79
Farnsfield, 80
Featherwood, 22, 61, 81
Fell End, 61, 80
Fendoch, 35
field fortification, Greek, 4
Forts,
    defence of, 47-48
    garrisons in, 35-54
    granaries, 48, 49, 85
    horses in, 37
    legionary, 42
    on Hadrian's Wall, 51-53
    paradigm for, 35
    vexilation, 41
Fortlets,
    definition of, 45
    defence of, 47-48
    on the Antonine Wall, 54
    on Hadrian's Wall, 51-53
Fortress, legionary,
    paradigm for, 46
Fosse Way, 55
Frontinus, Julius, 59

G

Gaeticuli, 29, 73
Gelligaer, 38
geometric mean, 21
Gergovia. 67
Gleadthorpe, 60, 80
Glenwhelt Leazes, 58, 79
Gloucester, 46
Golden Fleece, 58, 79
golden section, 23
Gosbecks, 42
Granaries, 48, 49, 85
Grange Moat, 58
Grassy Walls, 64, 65
Greenlee Lough, 79
Greensforge, 39, 40, 59, 81
Grindon Hill, 79
Grindon School, 58, 79
groma, 8, 15, 71
gromatici, 8, 71

H

Hadrian, emperor, 52
    British garrison under, 61, 62, 63
Hadrian's Wall, 43, 51, 54, 55
    garrison, 62, 63
Halton Chesters, 51, 52, 53, 62
Haltwhistle Burn, 58, 79
Hannibal, 4
Hardknott, 45
harmonic mean, 21
hastati, 11, 13
Hayton, York, 38
Heidenheim, 43, 44
Heraclea, 4
Hertfordshire, 55
Highstones, 45
Hippodamus of Miletus, 5
Hoole, 58
horses, in forts, 36, 37
Horstead, 55, 80
hospital
    in camp, 70, 74
    veterinary, 70, 74
hostages, 72
Housesteads, 51, 52, 53, 62
Hyginus, 3, 21, 25, see Appendix One
    Richmond's dating of, 77

I

Ilkley, 38
Inchtuthil, 46, 60, 80
Innerpeffray, 64, 65
Intervallum
    in camps, 6
    at Fendoch, 35
    in forts, 35
    in fortresses, legionary, 46
    at Numantia 17
    in the Hyginian camp, 30

J

Josephus, 3, 15, 56
Jugurthine War, 56

K

Kair House, 65

Katwijk, 48
Kent, 55
Keswick, 61
Kintore, 30, 65
Kinvaston, 41
Kirkbride, 40
Kirkby Thore, 60, 79, 80
Knowe Farm, 79

L

Lancaster, 41
Langwathby, 58, 79
Lantonside, 45
Learmouth, East, 59, 81
Lees Hall, 58, 60, 79
Legionary fortress, see Fortress
Legionary army groups, 59, 60
Lincolnshire, 55
Livy, 10
Llwyn y Brain, 41
London, 41
Longthorpe, 42
Loughor, 40
Lyne, 41, 43

M

Malham, 60, 80
Manchester, 40
maniples, 14
manpower
    for camp construction, 6, 15
    for defence of forts, 47, 48
Markham Cottage, 79, 81
Maryport, 62
Marius, 10
Masada, 3, 21, 30, 58
mathematics, Greek and Roman, 9, 21
Mauritanii, 29, 72,, 73
Mentieth, 60, 64, 80
Melandra, 38
metatores, 9
Metellus Pius, 19
Milestone House, 60, 80
Miletus, 5
Milrighall, 80
Misenum marines, 29, 30, 72, 73
Mons Graupius, 59
Moresby, 62
Moss Side, 58, 61, 79, 80

Muiryfold, 30, 65
Mumrills, 54

N

Newcastle upon Tyne, 52, 62
Newstead, 41, 43, 44, 45, 64, 81
Niederbieber, 43, 44
Norfolk, 55
Normandykes, 30, 65
Northumberland, 55
Norton 59, 81
Notional cohorts
    definition of, 26-27
    relation to camp acreage, 30
    signatures in forts, 35, 51
Nottinghamshire, 55
Nowtler Hill, 58, 79
Numantia, 3, 16, 17, 21

O

Oathlaw, 65
Oberstimm, 38
Old Carlisle, 40
Old Kilpatrick, 54
Old Penrith, 38

P

Palmyrenes, 29, 73, 73, 77
Pannonians, 29, 72, 73, 77
peditates sociorum, 11
Peloponnesian War, 4
Pena Redonda, 16, 19
phalanx, 3
Plumpton Head, 61
Poltross Burn, 45
Polybius, 3, 4, 7, 10, 11, 12, 13, 14, 16, 17, 49
praefectus castrorum, 9, 67
praetentura, 70-77
praetoria, 71
praetorian troops, 27, 29, 30, 70, 71, 73, 77
praetorium, 8, 70, 71, 74
Prestatyn, 39
principes, 11,13
principia,12
Pumpsaint, 39
Punic Wars, 16
Pyrrhus, king of Epirus, 4

Pythagoras, 21, 23

Q

quaestorium, 72, 73
Quatt, 57, 58, 79
Quietus, Lucius, 77
Quintana, Via, 12, 72

R

Rae Dykes, 22, 63, 64, 65, 81
Ravenna marines, 29, 30, 72, 73
Renieblas, 16, 17, 18, 28, 29, 37
    barracks at, 17-19
retentura, 35, 70-77
Rey Cross, 61, 80
Rhine, River, 67
Ribchester, 39
Richmond, I. A., Sir, 25.
Rochester, High, 77
Roy, General, 3
Rudchester, 51, 52, 53, 62

S

Sagularis, Via, 70, 71, 72, 73, 74
St Harmon, 60, 80
St Joseph, J.K., 3
St Leonard's, 81
Sallust, 56
scamnum, 71
Schulten, Adolf, 3, 16, 19
Scipio Aemilianus, 4
Scotland, large camps in, 63-65
scouts, 29
Seatsides, 60, 80
Severus, S., emperor, 64
Shropshire, 55
Silloans, 81
Sills Burn, 23, 58, 79
Silures, 59
Simpson, F.G., 25
Simpson, G., 25
Somerset, 55
space allowances,
    in forts, 35, 38-45, 47
    at Numantia, 17, 18
    original, 7
    in the Polybian camp, 13
    in Hadrian's Wall forts, 53
    in Antonine Wall forts, 54
    in the Hyginian camp, 26, 27
Spain, Roman army in, 16-19
speculatores, 73
spreadsheets, 31, 35, 56-57
stables in forts, 37
Staffordshire, 55
Stainmore, 61
Stanegate, 61
Stanwix, 43, 44, 52, 53, 62, 85, 86
statores, 29, 30
Stracathro, 21, 22, 61, 64, 81
Strageath, 38
Stretford Bridge, 38
Sunny Rigg, 58, 79
surveying, 7
Swindon, 61, 81
Swine Hill, 58, 79, 80
Syracuse, 4

T

Tacitus, 48, 59
Tawton, North, 40
tituli, 21
Trajan, emperor, 77
triarii, 11, 13
tribunes, military, 74
Troutbeck, 38, 58, 61, 79, 80, 81
turma(e), 7, 11, 14, 25, 43
Twice Brewed, 79

U

Uffington, 23, 61, 81
Upton, 60
Usk, 46

V

Valkenburg, 38, 48
Vegetius, 3, 8, 31, 32, 59
Vetera, 48
Vexillarii, 29, 30
Vindolanda, 39, 40

W

Wales, 59

Walford, 60, 80
Wall, 38
Wallsend, 51, 52, 53, 62
Walwick Fell, 58, 79
Warcop, 79
Watercrook, 38
Wath, 60, 80
Weisbaden, 40
Whitley Castle, 3
Willowford, 58, 79
Woodburn, West, 80
Woodhead, 80
Workshop, in camp, 70, 74
Wroxeter, 55

Y

Yardhope, North, 80
York, 46
Yorkshire, 55, 61
Ythan Wells, 64, 65